THE APOCALYPSE OF JESUS CHRIST

An Interpretation of
Our Saviour's Second Advent
"With Power and Great Glory"

by

M. P. Krikorian

DORRANCE & COMPANY

Philadelphia

Dedicated to the memory
of my sister Martha,
who loved "His Appearing"
and in that "Blessed Hope"
clung to her Bible as she
drank the Cup of Martyrdom.

CONTENTS

Page

Also by M. P. Krikorian:
The Spirit of the Shepherd
The Adjective of Antioch
The Prayer for the Prayerless
Is Man Lost?

FOREWORD

The Reverend M. P. Krikorian, author of this volume, has the advantage of having spent his earliest years and youth in a land not far from "those holy fields, over whose acres walked those blessed feet, which nineteen hundred years ago were nailed for our advantage on the bitter cross."

Now out of a long experience in the Gospel ministry, with an eloquence that uplifts the spirit of the reader, and a scholarly care that adds a peculiar dignity to his approach, he has addressed himself to a consideration of that "one far-off Divine event towards which the whole creation moves," the final epiphany of the God-Man on the soil of the earth, where once He walked in a visit of great humility and at length, in the sublime phrase of Sir W. Robertson Nicoll, "as our Eternal High Priest offered up the evening sacrifice of the world."

The book is redolent with the author's love of and fidelity to the Holy Scriptures. It is comprehensive in its presentation of the many facets of the cataclysmic coming of the Lord at the end of time. It is moving in style as it inspires with the contemplation of what the New Testament pronounces that "Blessed Hope" of Christ's Church.

Ministers, in particular, will find here source material in the best literary style for preaching on the subject to which the New Testament devotes more references than to the Incarnation itself. Lay students of the Word of God and the faith of the Church will find a study, devoid of technicality and written in a limpid manner, which they can readily grasp.

I recommend for wide reading this volume of the momentous theme from the pen of my dedicated and Christian friend and brother in Christ, the author, whose vivid expressive style achieves the end and aim of sound spiritual literature—to make his readers see the supreme urgency of the world-embracing truth and doctrinal depth of the Lord Jesus Christ's Coming Again.

The Reverend Galbraith Hall Todd, D.D.
Arch Street Presbyterian Church
Philadelphia

PREFACE

While in the midst of authoring this work, we had an occasion of sharing the Christian hospitality of a veteran Armenian minister and family in the friendly atmosphere of their home. During our season of fellowship, following the breaking of bread together, he extended the courtesy of introducing to me the manuscript of his proposed book: "A Voice from the Other World."

Although the intriguing title and its unique development held, in God's scheme, the promise of devotional literature of vital interest, the limited material had ample room for extension so as to command the consideration of a publisher. Accordingly, an idea presented itself and I ventured the suggestion: why not extend this message by adding a chapter on the important doctrine of Christ's Second Coming? Thereupon, he negotiated to his study and returning with a rather large book in the Armenian language, "Avedaranee Soolkher," "The Gospel Lights," published in Beirut, Lebanon; opened to a chapter, "Deru Ghergin Beedy Kah"—"The Lord is Coming Again."

Though my mastery and knowledge of the Armenian tongue, a noble language with exquisite phrases, capable of infinite development, leave much to be desired, I volunteered to translate for him from the Armenian into English the chapter on Christ's Second Coming; realizing very little that by so doing I was engaging myself to a full-orbed assignment. The chief difficulty, however, was not linguistic; the author's thoughts were lucid enough. But the translation asked of the translator, not only his mind, but his spirit and heart as well. Nevertheless, for all the labor entailed, it has been a rich and rewarding experience.

The present work, already well advanced before this task of

translation, represents its completion in the following pages. This modest addition to the eschatological literature is not an exhaustive exposition of the great doctrine of Christ's Second Coming, but an evangelical interpretation and discussion of the vital subject of the Christian hope. All apocalyptic believers and thoughtful Christians universally know that the end of Christ's mission and work is not yet; so they look forward to the great issue as the absolutely necessary event of the future. "He will come again with glory to judge the quick and the dead."

Our Lord Jesus Christ's Incarnation, Passion, Resurrection, Ascension and Session at the right hand of God the Father Almighty, all of which with supreme significance, being accomplished facts in themselves, point forward to the inevitable issue of His return to this world. He is coming again to manifest the judgment and righteousness of God, not only to individuals, but to the Church, to the nations, to the Messianic House of Israel and to the whole world of battle and blood! Everything demands this day of judgment. The cosmic Creation demands it; undeserved wrongs and injustices suffered without regard to the souls of an innumerable company of oppressed and dispossessed men and martyrs who are objects of divine mercy demand it; aye, the very character of the most high demands it also.

There is no greater and gladder promise in all the Word of God than the final word of Jesus to his Church, "Yea, I come quickly." It is the crown of all promise—the coronation of all evangelical hopes—the sum of all prophecy and prayer. Nature itself proclaims a Messiah coming again with power and great glory to rectify her unwilling disorders, to repair her shattered structures, to restore her oppressed energies, to vindicate her voice of conscience long questioned and overlooked and to complete her indispensable appointed course.

To first-century Christians the expectation of Christ's return was more present and urgent than it is to contemporary Christianity. And this expectation of His immediate return grew so intense that it required apostolic regulation. When the English historian, Edward Gibbon, singled out five natural causes by which he would account for the wide and rapid promulgation of Christianity, he enumerated as one, and not the least efficacious, the strong expectation entertained by early Christians of the Saviour's speedy return. Thus he displayed his acquaintance with the secret springs of action in the human heart for the greatest event. "The primitive Church thought more about the second coming of Jesus Christ than about death or heaven. The early Christians were looking not for a cleft in the ground called a grave, but for a cleavage in the sky called Glory. They were watching not for the 'undertaker' but for the 'Uppertaker.' " In an ever present eternity, how strange is the attitude of constant breaking away from this profound Biblical truth and doctrinal depth of Christ's Second Coming! Today, intentionally and often contemptuously His Return is regarded as a stumbling block to many in the Church of status quo, suspicious not only of her own historic faith, but who wall off the belief of others. How can the Church, "the pillar and ground of the truth," "the Church that waiteth for Thee," be so appallingly inarticulate? How can she speak only with stammering lips, and modify its intensity? Why should this expectation in this Gospel age grow less vivid when the history of mankind cries aloud for the day of revelation; when it is His Advent alone that will usher in "Thy Kingdom Come"—the Kingdom of peace—the ultimate meaning of history?

How haunting and peculiarly relevant in this connection is the poignant plaintive of the ancient Israelites for David, their banished monarch. "The King saved us . . . he delivered us: . . . Now therefore why speak ye not a word of bringing back the King?" (II Sam. 19:10). O Church, the Christian commonwealth and spiritual Israel of God, why speak ye not with ever enlarging commitment and spiritual imperative of Christ's coming back again?—"Christ who loved us, and saved us from our sins in his own blood." Assuredly, He could come back himself and will come with his victorious legions of angels, but his subjects are to urgently and earnestly speak the word for his coming. This work speaks that word. This interpretation is our declaration toward bringing back "the King of Kings, and Lord of Lords." And in this we are not alone, but in the glorious company of the ancient worthies of the Old and New Testaments—the holy men, organs of God's Spirit and Word, instruments of Christ, not content only to teach and explain, but also eager to win. These men of voltage, Moses and the Prophets, Patriarchs and Psalmists, "the Apostles of the Lord," Fathers of Church history and spiritual luminaries of all ages vigorously and unwaveringly spoke and wrote of the future appearance of Jesus Christ—the coming Messiah. The serious warning of the New Testament is that the day of seeming is over, the hour of reality is here at last. The Master is "at the door."

The aim and design of this book is to present a sound, simple and yet comprehensive Biblical view of this cosmic event of the future for the understanding and spiritual edification of those who have lived their lives in the context of the Christian Church, and desire the love of truth and divine knowledge but do not have time for the study of more profound works on this momentous subject. The author makes no reservation in this work. The material here contained is available to anyone who seeks the priceless treasure of all hopeful souls. "I believed, therefore have I spoken."

In sending forth this modest volume, I wish to record my gratitude to my lady of blue eyes for her kind support of not only typing the various drafts with exemplary diligence and persevering devotion but for her many indispensably helpful suggestions throughout.

This preface would not be complete without the author's grateful acknowledgment to the Reverend Dr. G. Hall Todd, eminent minister of the renowned Arch Street Presbyterian Church in Philadelphia, Pennsylvania: himself an evangelical scholar and a faithful dispenser of the Word of God and testimony of Jesus Christ; who, in spite of the pressing responsibilities of a metropolitan pulpit, found time to read the manuscript and shared its message and mission by a salutary foreword which it is hoped will play no small part in launching this subject of vital interest. I am also indebted to the eschatological company of devout and disciplined souls who loved "His Appearing," and with whom I have communed (some of whom are best known in heaven, whose shadows linger and whose fellowship endures), in search of exalting the One and only soul-satisfying Hope—Christ's Coming Again. And to that hope, I earnestly add my prayer that this message in print may quicken in my esteemed readers a great fondness for widening horizons, looking for that blessed hope and glorious appearing of the great God and our Saviour, Jesus Christ. Amen.

THE APOCALYPSE OF JESUS CHRIST

"I will come again"—Jesus—(St. John 14:3). "The Son of man cometh with power and great glory" (St. Matt. 24:29-31). "The Son of man cometh in the glory of his Father with the holy angels" (St. Mark 8:38). "He shall appear" (I John 3:2). "Behold he cometh with clouds" (St. John—Rev. 1:7). "The Lord himself shall descend from heaven with a shout, with the voice of the archangel and with the trump of God" (St. Paul—I Thess. 4:16). "The glorious appearing of the great God and our Saviour Jesus Christ" (St. Titus 2:13). "At the appearing of Jesus Christ," "when the chief Shepherd shall appear, ye shall receive a crown of glory that fadeth not away" (St. Peter 1:7; 5:4)

One of the two supreme facts of Christian history is that Jesus Christ the Eternal Son of God has been in this world (St. Matt. 1:18-25). And as there has been one appearing of Christ which is the object of believers' faithful and loving remembrance, there is to be another which is the object of our hopeful anticipation. Just as on the occasion of the First Coming of our Lord, there were those who were expecting and waiting for the consolation of Israel like devout and Spirit-filled Simeon; and aged prophetess and temple dweller like Anna who recognized him and proclaimed him as the Messiah to all them that looked for redemption in Jerusalem; just as a man of honorable estate who looked and waited for the Kingdom of God like Joseph of Arimathea; so because the time of His Second Appearing is fast approaching, we speak of the First and Second Advents of our Lord. In his address on the Second Advent at the Prophetical Conference in London, May 7, 1873, the Right Honorable, the Earl of Cavan declared: "Now I believe that Lord's people at the present day ought to be in a similar expectant and waiting attitude, looking for the speedy personal and pre-millennial advent of our blessed Lord."

In his book, *Why I Preach the Second Coming?* Pennsyl-

1

vania-born Dr. I. M. Haldeman declared: "The Second Coming of our Lord Jesus Christ is the one event most often recorded in Holy Scripture. It is recorded in type, in figure, in symbol, in analogue, in parable, in hyperbole and metaphor, in exalted song, in noblest poetry, in rarest rhetoric. It is set before us in dramatic and dynamic statement, in high prophetic forecast, in simple narrative, close-linked logic, expanded doctrine, divine exhortation and far-reaching appeal. It is bound up with every fundamental doctrine: the resurrection from the dead, the transfiguration of the living, the judgment seat of Christ, the judgment of the living nations, the consequent judgment of the white throne, the rewards of the righteous, the punishment of the wicked.

It is bound up with every sublime promise: the recognition of the dead, the overthrow of Satan, the deliverance of creation, the triumph of God and Christ, the eternal felicity of the saints.

So with great fondness for widening horizons we look for that blessed hope, and the glorious appearing of the great God and our Saviour Jesus Christ. The First Coming was for the salvation of sinners' *souls,* (St. Luke 19:10). The Second Coming is for the salvation of saints' *bodies,* to raise the deceased from their graves and to transfigure and translate to their rightful inheritance His waiting people, who shall then be living on the earth, to meet Him in the heavens, and gather them all together into His presence in one united and glorified company to be glorified in them and be admired in all of them that believe on Him: for there can be no resurrection of the body until our Lord Jesus Christ comes back. These two Advents, therefore, are the two chief moments in the history of the world, and give supernatural character to all revealed Christianity. At the commencement of the Christian year, the Church commemorates the First Advent and looks forward to the Second.

The glorious hope of all Christians, as was in the whole life of the apostolic Church, rests upon this unmistakable fact and divinely ordained truth that Jesus Christ is coming back again.

His pledge of return is sure; based upon the solid unshakable rock of historical fact, and sustained by the testimony of credible witnesses. He will some day reenter this planet! where He left His calling and credit card—the Church. From time immemorial, when the Council of Nicaea promulgated the ancient Nicean Creed, at 325 in Asia Minor crowds of Christians have been confessing at worship every Lord's Day the doctrine that Jesus Christ "shall come again with glory, to judge the quick and the dead."

"Greatest week," exulted the president of the United States, Richard Nixon, "in the history of the world since Creation," as he welcomed, in words of praise the three astronauts, Neil Armstrong, Edwin Aldrin and Michael Collins on the deck of the U.S.S. *Hornet* in mid-Pacific on July 24, 1969, who had just returned from a successful Apollo 11 mission to the moon.

This transcendent event of one of the brightest hours of man's achievement has been called the greatest feat in history. While Apollo 11's awesome accomplishment marks a most significant and dramatic event before the world, greater ones than this tower as the pillars and ground of history. They are the events of the Garden of Eden—Creation of man; the dimlit Manger—Incarnation of Jesus Christ which still divides history into B.C. and A.D.; the bloodstained Cross—Crucifixion; the empty tomb—the Resurrection; and the greatest event of them all is the Trump of God—Revelation which will embrace Christ's Coming with power and great glory.

All above events including the Apollo 11 mission are, to the celebrated body preparation and signs of this cosmic event of the future; the Son of Man's Coming; the consummation of history; the final drama in man's redemption; the establishment of His Kingdom and the investiture of the saints in their future sovereignties.

> For the grace of God that bringeth salvation hath appeared to all men,
> Teaching us that, denying ungodliness and worldly lusts,

we should live soberly, righteously, and godly, in this present world;

Looking for that blessed hope, and the glorious appearing of the great God and our Saviour Jesus Christ; (St. Titus 2:11-13).

Beloved, now are we the sons of God, and it doth not yet appear what we shall be: but we know that, when we shall appear, we shall be like him; for we shall see him as he is.

And every man that hath this hope in him purifieth himself, even as he is pure. (I John 3:2-3).

Wherefore comfort one another with these words (I Thess. 4:18).

He which testifieth these things saith, Surely I come quickly. Amen. Even so, come, Lord Jesus. (Rev. 22:20).

It is an historically clear and established fact that the Second Coming of the Lord Jesus Christ is a fundamental tenet of Christian religion and Biblical Christianity. The Coming of Jesus Christ, an oft-repeated doctrine, with towering prominence in the Holy Scriptures, indeed over three hundred times in the 260 chapters of the New Testament, more in number than its pages, attested to by the unimpeachable witnesses of the apostolic band above, shines as the great star and hope of the Church. Nor is there another subject upon which more stress is laid in all the Word of God. In Biblical exegesis and in the all-controlling conception of scriptural exposition whenever a subject is mentioned so frequently as Christ's Second Coming, it speaks and emphasizes its cosmic importance and tangible reality. The Lord Jesus Christ is coming again to receive His own and will come in the glory of the Father with the holy angels. This, to repeat, is the pole star of the hope of the Church; the perfection of his charismatic bond. It is not only the hope but the crowning comfort of all believers who anchor their redemptive trust in Him. The Lord Jesus Christ is coming again, not in humiliation, but in glory; not in weakness, but in power; not to suffer, but to reign! And when we think of all the attendant circumstances which are predicted—the Rapture of the Saints, the descent of the Lord from heaven, the Divine Judgment, the binding of Satan, the renewal of this earth, and all those sublimely majestic scenes to be produced by His glory; who can contemplate this awesome subject of Christian hope without feeling his spirit subdued and solemnized, without feeling that we have presented to us in the Holy Scriptures one of the grandest and most glorious objects which it is possible for the mind of mortal man to conceive; that upon which our hope is to rest, that toward which our expectations are to tend? Although this Biblical narration of the Last Things and prospect of a return of Christ accompanied by the transformation of this world order, a final judgment and vindication of the sovereignty of God over heaven and earth, is regarded as incredibly fantastic by the scientific humanist of the twentieth century; although many have lost valid grounds for believing in this doctrine of cosmic eschatology, we who believe in this apocalyptic age "are not of them who draw back . . . ; but of them that believe" (Heb. 10:39).

"Grace be unto you, and peace, from him which is, and which was, and which is to come" (Rev. 1:4). Did the Lord Jesus Christ complete His work on earth during His first advent and leave to secondary agents and spiritual influences the finishing of His great plan of redemption, or did He simply accomplish the first stage of that great work and His coming back again in person to this old earth will complete that glorious plan? "It is not God's way to do things by halves." We are not orphans of eternity.

The Lord's return to earth to complete His divinely ordained plan and to establish His Kingdom for which the believers pray, is: Christians' shining hope (I John 3:3): the hope of the Church (St. Titus 2:13): the hope of Israel (Rom. 11:26): the hope of the nations (Hag. 2:7): and the hope of creation. For this created universe waits with eager expectation for God's son to be revealed because the universe itself is to be delivered from the shackles of mortality and to enter upon the glorious liberty and splendor of the children of God (Rom. 8:21-22). Christ's Second Coming was the proper end-point of history. Hope for the future is the only transcendence in the universe: where there is hope, there is a dynamic life in Christ. The Bible certifies it. God guarantees it.

I

WHAT THE APOCALYPSE OF
THE LORD JESUS CHRIST IS

Not Death. One of the common and most popular beliefs is, that Christ's Second Coming is fulfilled at a believer's death; that at death the coming of the Lord is practically realized by each one individually. In speaking to the Thessalonian Christains about their loved ones who had passed on, the apostle does not comfort them by saying the Lord has come for them, but comforts them by their apocalyptic hope, saying the Lord is coming for them. The private coming of the Lord at death of saints cannot be His Second Coming, because saints are dying every day.

Recently, it was my solemn mission to officiate at the funeral of a dear friend, who, after a prolonged illness, finished his course on this mortal sphere. Throughout his weeks of valiant and patient suffering, watching and waiting, frequent prayers were offered both at his bedside and more often by telephone in which he always joined with whispers of "Amen." During his last ten minutes before his soul took wings to higher glory he held both hands high up above his head beckoning to the Saviour whom he beheld moving toward him. With a sublime sense of the future, in true discernment and sure confidence he prayed the apostle's apocalyptic prayer: "Come, Lord Jesus, come, come quickly."

The prayer was answered and with a last whisper of an "Amen"—so be it—on his lips, he had an abundant entrance into his inheritance in the everlasting Kingdom of our Lord and Saviour, Jesus Christ. Death to such a good man at any time is a greater beatitude than a disaster; and when a life of truth and honor becomes so great a suffering as at this time, it is a blessedness to have it ended. The cessation of blood through an inert body, stopping the heart and brain wave which completes the process of living, cannot be Christ's Second Coming. Moreover, as noted in above passages, the Son of Man cometh in power and great glory, in the glory of his Father with the holy angels and archangels and with the trump of God (St. Mark 8:38; I Thess. 4:16). At the death of the believers the Lord does not come in this dramatic and dynamic form. The disciples did not think that the Coming of the Lord meant death. There can be no death where He is.

Then again, because death is an enemy; "The last enemy that shall be destroyed is death" (I Cor. 15:26). Death separates us from our loved ones and friends; the Lord's coming reunites us. Death is the curse of sin; Lord's coming removes the curse of sin forever. If Christ's second coming is death, what was His first coming? "If I go I will come again." Who is the "I" in the first instance; who is the "I" in the second? According to this revised version, the passage should read, "If I go away, death will come again." Very awkward and untenable theology, to say the least, and not worthy to be ranked with "rightly dividing the word of truth." His Coming is not death but resurrection. He is the Resurrection and the Life.

Not Our Going To Him. He comes for us (St. John 14:3).

Recently there passed away from this mortal sphere one of the world's most celebrated musical maestros, Sir Malcolm Sargent of Great Britain. During an interview with the general secretary of the American Bible Society, (at the one hundred fiftieth anniversary of the society he had conducted with superb skill an unforgettable performance of Handel's mighty oratorio, "The Messiah"), Sir Malcolm spoke with deep reverence of the descent of the Holy Spirit upon the concert hall (as the strains rose heavenward), and of the Lord's coming. In a tribute to the brave and brilliant man of God who shortly after finished his earthly course, the secretary closed his tribute saying: "And the Lord came for him in

October 3, 1967." While we cannot identify the death of believers with the final coming of Jesus Christ, there is a coming of Christ to every believer as in the case of Sir Malcolm at the time of his death. So in the same act the great musician went to Him where he might be swaying the immortal baton.

Not The Holy Spirit. Who is another spiritual indwelling.

> But the Comforter, which is the Holy Ghost, whom the Father will send in my name, he shall teach you all things, and bring all things to your remembrance, whatsoever I have said unto you (St. John 14:26).

"We shall be like him; for we shall see him as he is (I John 3:2). Who dares to reason that Saint John did not have the Lord in his heart as deeply as any modern saints, yea, infinitely more so. Have any would-be modern saints gotten closer to Christ than Saint Paul, a man twice made in the image of God? Yet it was he who said; We "shall be caught up together" (I Thess. 4:17). "Paraclete" and "Parousia" have been needlessly confused by more than one writer, the "Paraclete" which constantly occurs in the Holy Scriptures as describing our Lord's Second Coming has been applied in some learned works to the advent of the Holy Spirit at Pentecost. The truth is, the entire New Testament was written after Pentecost, and declares no less than 150 times that the Second Coming of the Lord Jesus Christ was still in the future. Moreover, none of the great events predicted as accompanying the Second Coming occurred at the descent of the Holy Spirit on the day of Pentecost, such as the Resurrection of the "Dead in Christ," and the translation of the "Living Saints."

Let us observe the difference. In the "paraclete," Christ comes spiritually and invisibly. In the "Parousia," He comes bodily and gloriously. The Advent of the Holy Spirit is really conditioned on the Saviour's personal departure from His people (St. John 16:7). His Second Coming, on the other hand, is only realized in His personal return to His people (I Thess. 2:19). The Holy Spirit attends the Church in the days of her humiliation: the Second Coming introduces the Church into the day of her glory. In the Holy Spirit, Christ came to dwell with the Church on earth (St. John 14:18). In the Second Coming He takes the Church to dwell with himself in glory (St. John 14:3). Christ prayed in behalf of His bereaved Church for the coming of the Holy Spirit (St. John 14:16). The blessed Holy Spirit now prays with the pilgrim Church for the hastening of His Second Coming (Rev. 22:17).

Not Spiritual Coming to Each at Conversion. The diffusion of Christianity and spread of the Gospel cannot be the Second Coming of the Lord; because the dissemination of Christianity is gradual, while the "Return of the Lord" shall be sudden, as a thief in the night (St. Matt. 24:27, 42, 44; I Thess. 5:2; Rev. 3:3). Then again the spread of the Gospel and Christianity is a progressive and forward movement, whereas the "Return of the Lord" is a monumental *event;*

> And while they looked steadfastly toward heaven as he went up, behold, two men stood by them in white apparel;
> Which also said, Ye men of Galilee, why stand ye gazing up into heaven? this same Jesus, which is taken up from you into heaven shall so come in like manner as ye have seen him go into heaven" (Acts 1:10-11).

This was the very last message of the ascending Lord Jesus Christ; his specific subject as He hovered in midair between earth and heaven. His parting word was sent back by the angelic messengers who stood by the enraptured disciples saying, "Why stand ye gazing up into heaven? This same Jesus shall so come again in like manner as ye have seen him go into heaven." When a highly noted theologian and ecclesiastic was asked: "Do you think Christ in any literal sense will come back?" he replied: "My only honest answer is, I do not and I cannot know." The angels knew. Put this cluster of the letter

10

'S' together, *same, shall, so* and *seen* and you have a fourfold infallible proof of the Lord Jesus Christ's return: *personally, literally* and *visibly* as He departed. The Scriptural meaning of the Apocalypse of Jesus Christ is His future reappearance, clothed with the honors and crowned with the triumphs which are to characterize that forthcoming, and not mere knowledge or description of this great theme. And it is that Apocalypse, that Revelation of Jesus Christ, with all its glorious concomitants, that God has in covenant given to Christ;—given to Him as the crowning reward of His mediatorial work.

II

PROPHETIC WITNESSES OF CHRIST'S COMING

The prophets are witnesses of His coming.

Enoch also, the seventh from Adam, prophesied of these saying, "Behold, the Lord cometh with ten thousands of His Saints" (St. Jude 14). This precious fragment from a prophet of antediluvian age, the earliest Biblical revelation by one who is described as walking with God, the Creator; has come and is ever coming. Eternal God, embracing in a glance the keyboard of sixty centuries, touches by turns, with the finger of the Spirit—and lays his left hand on Enoch, the seventh from Adam, and his right hand on John the Apostle, the loving and sublime prisoner of Patmos. From the one strain is heard: "Behold the Lord cometh with ten thousand of his saints," from the other: "Behold, he cometh with the clouds!" And between the notes of this Messianic hymn of three thousand years there is eternal harmony and the angels stoop to listen; the elect of God are moved and eternal life descends into the souls of men. How divinely significant it is that most ancient recorded prophecy should begin with that with which the last Old Testament prophet ends the ancient literature of Israel, and with which the prophet of Patmos also closes the New Testament. "Behold, the Lord cometh" says Enoch; "The Lord whom ye seek shall suddenly come" ends prophet Malachi. Enoch was not a Hebrew prophet. He lived and prophesied long before Moses and the law. It was through his ministry that a seed was prepared to survive the fearful flood to become the heads and princes of the repeopled earth. The son of Sirach celebrates him as taken up alive to heaven, that he might be a teacher and a witness. Such a token and witness he was in his own time. Patriotic poetry sings of him as the "signal ornament" of the Patriarchal Church, who by counsel strove to recall peoples gone astray from God. With pungency and fire he prophesied of the fearful coming of the Lord to execute judgment upon all, for all their hard speeches and ungodly deeds. (Jude 14, 15).

Job. An eminently religious soul, in that amazing drama in the book with poetic license which bears his name, experienced the primacy and tragedy of undeserved human suffering. He who had so little to comfort him in this present world, comforts himself with the believing hopes of happiness in the next world by his prophetic confession and sublime faith in the Living and Coming Christ. In an awesome faculty of choice and a depth of consciousness unknown to profane man, such as his vexing visitors, he replies:

> For I know that my redeemer liveth, and that he shall stand at the latter day upon the earth;
> And though after my skin worms destroy this body, yet in my flesh shall I see God:
> Whom I shall see for myself, and mine eyes shall behold, and not another; (Job 19:25-27).

In the face of staggering loss of health, wealth and family, it was not easy for the Patriarch of Uz, the Idumean desert dweller, to keep on believing in one God while surrounded with sun and moon worshippers, whose adoration he had been invited to share. But for him there was only one God, Eloah, the Lofty One to whom he clung with deepening faith and surpassing genius. Therefore, his latter days, under Jehovah's blessing as reward and restoration for his heroic resolution and immovable contempt of suffering and death, proved that it was good to believe.

David was a devout worshipper who had the prophetic understanding of Yahveh as the Lord of holiness. He was a psalmist of profound spiritual experience, a great statesman, soldier, saint and constructor of the Judean kingdom, which today has found greatness in politics and history. Looking ahead with an apocalyptic insight to the Messianic Kingdom of Christ, in a great Hebraic hymn of high thoughts, he caught a glimpse of the golden age—the glories of that Kingdom of universal government, judgment, joy and rejoicing.

O worship the Lord in the beauty of holiness: fear before him, all the earth.

Say among the heathen that the Lord reigneth: the world also shall be established that it shall not be moved: he shall judge the people righteously.

Let the heavens rejoice, and let the earth be glad; let the sea roar, and the fulness thereof.

Let the fields be joyful, and all that is therein: then shall all the trees of the wood rejoice

Before the Lord: for he cometh, for he cometh to judge the earth: he shall judge the world with righteousness, and the people with his truth.

The Lord reigneth; let the earth rejoice; let the multitude of isles be glad thereof. (Ps. 96:9-13, 97:1).

Daniel is a prophetic witness of Christ's Second Coming.

I saw in the night visions, and, behold, one like the son of man came with the clouds of heaven, and came to the Ancient of days, and they brought him near before him.

And there was given him dominion, and glory, and a kingdom, that all people, nations, and languages, should serve him: his dominion is an everlasting dominion, which shall not pass away, and his kingdom that which shall not be destroyed (Daniel 7:13-14).

Here is the scene in heaven before the Coming of the Son of Man.

I beheld till the thrones were cast down, and the Ancient of days did sit, whose garment was white as snow, and the hair of his head like the pure wool: his throne was like the fiery flame, and his wheels as burning fire.

A fiery stream issued and came forth from before him:

14

thousand thousands ministered unto him, and ten thousand
times ten thousand stood before him: the judgment was set,
and the books were opened. (Daniel 7:9-10).

The Lord Jesus Christ Himself is a prophet of His Coming.

Jesus saith unto him, Thou hast said: nevertheless I say
unto you,
Hereafter shall ye see the Son of man sitting on the right
hand of power, and coming in the clouds of heaven. (St.
Matt. 26:64).
Immediately after the tribulation of those days shall the
sun be darkened, and the moon shall not give her light, and
the stars shall fall from heaven, and the powers of the
heavens shall be shaken:
And then shall appear the sign of the Son of man in
heaven: and then shall all the tribes of the earth mourn, and
they shall see the Son of man coming in the clouds of heaven
with power and great glory.
And he shall send his angels with a great sound of a
trumpet, and they shall gather together his elect from the
four winds, from one end of heaven to the other. (St. Matt.
24:29-31).

Consider now, how did He go? He was taken up in a cloud;
He was taken literally; He was taken personally; He was taken
visibly. And this same Jesus who was taken will return as
personally, literally and visibly as He departed. If this language does not mean what it says, then there is no way of
knowing what it means. To the honest student and seeker
after truth as revealed and recorded in the Word of God, the
sense is as clear as the meridian sun, so that "the wayfaring
men, though fools, shall not err therein."
The Angels are prophets of His Second Coming, and they
were not mistaken at His *First* Coming (Acts 1:10-11).
"The Apostles of the Lord" are the prophetic witnesses of
His Coming and repeatedly spoke under the Divine direction

of the Holy Spirit.

The Apostle Paul:

But I would not have you to be ignorant, brethren, concerning them which are asleep, that ye sorrow not, even as others which have no hope.

For if we believe that Jesus died and rose again, even so them also which sleep in Jesus will God bring with him.

For this we say unto you by the word of the Lord, that we which are alive and remain unto the coming of the Lord shall not prevent them which are asleep.

For the Lord himself shall descend from heaven with a shout, with the voice of the archangel, and with the trump of God: and the dead in Christ shall rise first:

Then we which are alive and remain shall be caught up together with them in the clouds, to meet the Lord in the air: and so shall we ever be with the Lord.

Wherefore comfort one another with these words. (I Thess. 4:13-18)

Henceforth there is laid up for me a crown of righteousness, which the Lord, the righteous judge, shall give me at that day: and not to me only, but unto all them also that love his appearing (II Tim. 4:8).

For as often as ye eat this bread, and drink this cup, ye do show the Lord's death till he come (I Cor. 11:26).

For our conversation is in heaven; from whence also we look for the Saviour, the Lord Jesus Christ (Phil. 3:20).

So Christ was once offered to bear the sins of many; and unto them that look for him shall he appear the second time without sin unto salvation (Heb. 9:28).

The Apostle Peter:

But the day of the Lord will come as a thief in the night; in the which the heavens shall pass away with a great noise, and the elements shall melt with fervent heat, the earth also and the works that are therein shall be burned up.

Seeing then that all these things shall be dissolved, what

manner of persons ought ye to be in all holy conversation and godliness,

Looking for and hasting unto the coming of the day of God, wherein the heavens being on fire shall be dissolved, and the elements shall melt with fervent heat?

Nevertheless we, according to his promise, look for new heavens and a new earth, wherein dwelleth righteousness.

Wherefore, beloved, seeing that ye look for such things, be diligent that ye may be found of him in peace, without spot and blameless (II Peter 3:10-14).

The Apostle John:

And now, little children, abide in him; that when he shall appear, we may have confidence, and not be ashamed before him at his coming (I John 2:28).

The Apostle James:

Be patient therefore, brethren, unto the coming of the Lord. Behold, the husbandman waiteth for the precious fruit of the earth, and hath long patience for it, until he receive the early and latter rain.

Be ye also patient; establish your hearts; for the coming of the Lord draweth nigh (James 5:7-8).

Fathers of Church History are the prophetic witnesses of our Lord's coming again. Hear these giants of apocalyptic faith and heroes of this blessed doctrine—the living monuments of sacred history:

Barnabus, Polycarp, Clement of Alexandria, Ignatius of Loyola, Tertullian, Justin Martyn, Nepos, Irenaus, Victorinus, Methodius, Hermas;

all were one on the subject of the Coming of our Lord Jesus Christ.

Modern Apostles are the prophetic witnesses of our Lord's coming back again. Listen to these pillars of the Church sounding forth the trumpet of this eschatological and glorious event as they speak to us on this side of the Reformation:

Martin Luther, John Calvin, John Knox, Tyndale, Baxter, Bunyan, Sir Isaac Newton, John and Charles Wesley, Whitefield, George Mueller, Charles G. Finney, A. T. Pierson, A. C. Gaeblein, Charles H. Spurgeon, D. L. Moody, A. C. Dixon, G. Campbell Morgan, Sir Robert Anderson, C. I. Schofield, Reuben Archer Torrey, James M. Gray, Philip Mauroo, W. H. Griffith Thomas and other cloud of witnesses in all ages of the Church which no man can number!

Finally: *The Lord's Supper* is a prophetic witness of His Coming.

For as often as ye eat this bread, and drink this cup, ye do show the Lord's death till he come (I Cor. 11:26).

It has been said: "The Lord's Supper is not a permanent ordinance. It will discontinue when the Lord returns. It is a memorial feast which looks back to the Cross and forward to the Coming. An engagement ring is not intended to be permanent. It is simply a pledge of mutual love which gives place to the wedding ring. So the Lord's Table may be looked upon as a betrothal pledge left to the Church during the absence of her betrothed."

"He cometh." Christ has not gone to heaven to stay there. He has gone for His Church's benefit; and for the Church's benefit He will return again; not in spirit only, not in Providence only, not in the removal of men by death as previously noted, but in His own person, as "the Son of Man." This is the immutable truth of God, predicted by his prophets above, promised by all of the apostles, believed by all early Christians, acknowledged in all of the Church Creeds, sung of in all of the Church hymn books, prayed about in all of the Church liturgies, and entering so essentially into the very life and substance of Christianity, that without it there can be no true Christianity. That Christianity that does not look for a returning Saviour, nor locate the highest and holiest hope and triumph in the judgment scenes for which the Son of Man must reappear, is not the Christianity of the Bible, and is without authority to promise the assurance of salvation to its devotees. Some may murmur at it, others may dispute it, still others may despise and mock at it and hide from it, notwithstanding, it is a great fundamental article of the Gospel of Christ whose Apocalypse is the crown of the inspired Canon. He is now at the right hand of God the Father Almighty, from thence He shall come to judge the quick and the dead.

III

THE TIME OF HIS ADVENT

To the contemplative question and entrancing quest of the disciples in His Olivet discourse, "When shall these things be? and what shall be the sign of thy coming, and of the end of the world?" Jesus gave this startling answer: "Of that day and hour knoweth no man, no, not the angels in heaven, but my Father only."

The Christian Church in general has supposed that this answer of Jesus meant that the time of the end and of the Second Coming of Christ is altogether hidden from believers' discovery. But the Holy Scriptures distinctly intimate that the time of the end shall be revealed to watchful Christians. "Surely the Lord GOD will do nothing but he revealeth his secret unto his servants" (Amos 3:7; St. John 15:15; I Thess. 5:4). Moreover, the answer of Jesus to this staggering concept and cosmic purpose of God's ineffable mystery was in the present tense before His ascension and glorification and before the descent of the Holy Spirit on the day of Pentecost. Therefore, the message and meaning of the Olivet text is beyond the present and in the future and it cannot be said that the Son does not know the day and the hour of His own coming.

The Church, the Bride of Christ can have her say on a date for her wedding only when she is assured that the Bridegroom has full knowledge of this day and hour of His Advent. He, "in whom are hid all the treasures of wisdom and knowledge," knows the day and hour of His Second Coming.

There are those who believe that a spiritual millennium is to come by the spread of the Gospel to all the world; to them, the Coming of Christ is the progress of modern civilization. The

20

glory of Christianity is to keep abreast with the times, to press popular education, to create machinery to reach and elevate the masses, to follow up conquest of arms with schools and civilization, to purify and influence legislation, to improve society by gradual reforms and general enlightenment, to win for the Church the patronage of the rich and great, and so to progress till the whole earth shall rest in the embrace of a spiritual kingdom. This popular teaching is called "post-millennialism." This doctrine is only about 250 years old, and was instituted by Daniel Whitby, an English clergyman, or proclaimed by him as a new hypothesis.

His "new hypothesis" was that by the preaching of the Gospel, Islamism, a legendary counterfeit and forgery of Judaism and Christianity, with its "lying divinations and vain deceit, after the tradition" of Mohammed, the self-avowed and awesomely fanatical Arabian imposter, would be overthrown, Judaism would be converted, and Hierarchial Catholicism would crumble away into nothingness, and this triumph of the Church would constitute the Millennium of a thousand years of righteousness and peace, culminating in the return of Christ. This would mean that Jesus would not come until after the Millennium.

A cursory examination of history seems to reveal that the age was ripe for this "new theory": this computerized *Te Deum*. Great Britain was in a religious fervor and excitement. The Great Evangelical Awakening followed under Whitefield and the Wesleys at the mercy of Divine Providence and was looked upon by Whitby as a mobile version of the Millennium about to be ushered in. The giant agony of the world with its eclipse of spiritual values and chaos, the heartbreak and tragedy of the human race since experienced in this mortal sphere and shaky cosmos eloquently demonstrated that Whitby was wrong.

Notwithstanding, incredible as it seems, his theory was widely and avidly received, and spread with uncommon speed until postmillennialism is known today as an established doctrine in Christendom, as a view of the cosmic drama of the Second Coming of Christ. It is worthy of note that post-millennialism as believed in our day is less than three centuries old, whereas premillennial belief dates back to not only the Apostolic Church of the first century, but to the profile of the prophetic days of Isaiah and Daniel, "the man greatly beloved."

The Holy Scriptures warrant no such conclusion of a Millennium by the spread of the Gospel as the triumph of the Church as the postmillennialists would have us believe. On the contrary, the Bible pictures that this age will not only wind up in human progress, but it will be the catastrophe of all earthly pomp and pride. The proud oaks and lofty cedars of the mountains of human conceit and self-will which will not have Christ to rule over them, will taste God's outpouring indignation. "As it was in the days of Noah, so shall it be when the Son of man shall be revealed." The great World Wars of the first half of the twentieth century, with their universal catastrophes and accompanying evils, deadly diseases and privation, have opened the eyes of many of these apostles who preach that the world is getting better.

The staggering appropriations to increase military might, the tortured problem of race and volatile tensions between white and black are threatening the world with disaster. Haunted by a sense of futility and frustration, there is, in the present posture of modern civilization and space age, a cup of overflowing anxiety brought about by the phenomenal and frightening findings of science. Dr. Geoffrey F. Fisher, when archbishop of Canterbury, as Britain's leading churchman, himself viewed in a gloomy and forbidding picture the ecumenical disaster of the human race and its hope for the future. The eminent ecclesiastic delivered the funeral oration of the nations by the uncomfortable doctrine, "it is within the Providence of God that the human race should wipe itself off the face of the earth, in an atomic and nuclear war." "He must indeed be blind who does not see *now* that these nations are under the leadership of Satan, the god of this age. All the unscriptural dreams of postmillennialism are ended. World conversion and rapidly advancing kingdoms making for universal righteousness can no longer be defended. GOD'S WORD IS VINDICATED. This age is an evil age. Its end is not peace and righteousness, but the opposite. . . . The beasts may be chained after awhile, but they will break loose again." They have broken loose, and that globally. That faith and system of philosophy that human nature and the world are improving is slowly and inexorably being destroyed by events, and something else is bound to take its place. That something else is the Coming of Christ.

What His Coming is. Christ's coming back to earth in "Power and great Glory" is both premillenial and imminent. Let us consider the meaning of the word, imminent. The word imminent from the Latin signifies, close at hand, with a sense of projecting and hanging over, liable to happen at once. By imminency therefore, we understand an event may happen at any time. Imminency however, does not necessarily imply immediateness, which means instantly; even the briefest interval or lapse of time which demands watchfulness.

When astronomer Johannes Kepler, after years of unremitting toil and many unsuccessful theories, but sustained by patient waiting and working, finally found the laws relative to the motions of the planets, he cried out, "O Almighty God, I am thinking Thy thoughts after Thee."

At the conversion of Zaccheus, the giant little-man of Jericho, who farmed the revenue for the Roman Empire, Jesus delivered a moving message on "Salvation." The impact of that discourse was so great that those early Palestinians thought "that the Kingdom of God should immediately appear." By the parables of "ten pounds," the Master teacher taught how men may think the thoughts of God; He charged them: "Occupy till I come." To occupy ourselves by an unconditional commitment to the proclamation of the Gospel and to bring the nations to the knowledge of Christ and to the obedience of Faith in a watchful expectation for His sky-rocketing return is to think God's thoughts after Him.

Free from undue dogmatism, it is safe to observe that at no period of the Church's history have the conditions necessary for the Lord's Return been so overwhelmingly fulfilled as at the present time. "He that hath an ear," let him hear what the imperative command of the Apocalyptic Angel was to the Son of Man, astride upon the "white cloud," as crying aloud he voiced, "Thrust in thy sickle, and reap: . . . for the harvest of the earth is ripe."

Now the term, premillennial. The premillennial view is that Christ must necessarily come back to earth in "Power and great Glory" before the "Thousand Years" of righteousness and universal peace as taught unequivocally in the Word of God (Rev. 20:1-6). "And I hold it to be clearly shown in Scripture," said the Earl of Cavan, "that the personal return of Christ will take place *before* the Millennium of a thousand years."

The coming of our Lord, as previously noted, is mentioned 316 times in 260 chapters of the New Testament; so the premillennial doctrine is not a hobby, a whim, a fad, nor is it a fantastic dream of deluded souls; but a born revelation conceived by the Holy Ghost within the bosom of every honest seeker of the truth.

Dr. J. H. Brooks tells us: "The premillennial advent was the common heritage of both the Jewish and the Gentile Christians, and passed from the Jewish Christian precisely in the way the Gospel passed."

Dr. Grattan Guiness, an equally eminent scholar, says: "It cannot be denied that for three centuries the Church had the Doctrine of the Premillennial coming of Christ." The very structure of the New Testament demands that Christ shall return before the Millennium. When He comes He will raise the dead, but the righteous dead are to be raised before the Millennium that they may reign with Christ during a thousand years: therefore there can be no Millennium before Christ comes. The Apostolic Church was preeminently Pre-Millennial, and for two centuries no other view was entertained. The writings of the Church Fathers abound in evidence of this fact. At the Reformation itself the doctrine of the premillennial return of the Lord was an outstanding emphasis—a revival point.

The Duke of Manchester, a nineteenth century author, in his treatise, "The Finished Mystery," argues in proof of the premillennial or millenarian view, that the personal return of Christ to this earth will take place just before the Millennium, and that Christ will visibly and personally reign over the earth during that period of a thousand years, which will, therefore, not be merely a spiritual Millennium, or improved condition of society by a universal spread of true Christianity, but will include in addition the actual bodily presence of Christ and His heavenly saints, continually visiting this earth in person, and holding intercourse with its mortal unglorified generations of mankind, like as God and the angels at times visibly appeared in former times to the patriarchs.

We would respect all students for their postmillennial views, albeit, we cannot refrain from reminding them that the Bible warrants no such conclusion of world righteousness through the spread of human progress and spiritual and ethical principles. On the contrary, the Holy Scriptures picture that the age will not wind up in human progress and advancement, but it will end in catastrophe (St. Matt. 24:36-39).

As in our mid-twentieth century and apocalyptic age in the process of collapsing, "the earth also was corrupt before God, and the world was filled with violence. God looked upon the earth, and behold, it was corrupt; for all flesh had corrupted his way upon the earth" (Gen. 6:11-12). The 120 years of Patriarch Noah's faithful warnings and preachings fell on deaf and scoffers' ears whose consciences were seared with hot iron—dead. The voice of God's chosen vessel was ignored by profane elements. But what of them? Their monumental epitaph upon the ageless tombstone reads: "All in whose nostrils was the breath of life, who defied the message of the dedicated messenger perished in the judgment of the Flood" (Gen. 7:21-23). God ordained rain, forty days and nights, that washed away the wicked and was the salvation of the righteous Father Noah and his family of eight souls. The highly honored poet-psalmist was close to the heart of truth when he sang: "The Lord knoweth the way of the righteous: but the way of the ungodly shall perish."

From the foregoing passages in the Gospel of St. Matthew and related Scriptures, it is transparently clear that the time of His coming is before the world is converted. In the meantime—the time of watching and waiting—is it possible for the humble believers who occupy till He comes to forecast, at least approximately, the time of His return? This, of course, does not mean that Scriptures warrant ambitious date-setting on the part of fallible men. Our position is not to foretell the Divine program in the future; but to be students of prophecy which God Himself has given in the light of history and Providence; God's own interpretation of His Word.

The book of Revelation encourages by a distinct benediction a careful study of the prophetic word, especially this particular book.

> Blessed is he that readeth, and they that hear the voice of this prophecy, and keep those things which are written therein: for the time is at hand (Rev. 1:3).

The prophet and seer of Patmos was instructed not to seal the word of his prophecy, for the time was at hand. The prophet Daniel on the contrary, 630 years before this was commanded to seal his prophecy, and he adds with pathos:

> And he said, Go thy way, Daniel: for the words are closed up and sealed till the time of the end.
> Many shall be purified, and made white, and tried; but the

wicked shall do wickedly (Daniel 12:9-10).

Imminent. At any hour. "Watch."

> Watch therefore: for ye know not what hour your Lord doth come.
> But know this, that if the goodman of the house had known in what watch the thief would come, he would have watched, and would not have suffered his house to be broken up.
> Therefore be ye also ready: for in such an hour as ye think not the Son of man cometh (St. Matt. 24:42-44).
> For the Son of man is as a man taking a far journey, who left his house, and gave authority to his servants, and to every man his work, and commanded the porter to watch.
> Watch ye therefore: for ye know not when the master of the house cometh, at even, or at midnight, or at the cock-crowing, or in the morning:
> Lest coming suddenly he find you sleeping.
> And what I say unto you I say unto all, Watch. (St. Mark 13:34-37).
> But of the times and the seasons, brethren, ye have no need that I write unto you.
> For yourselves know perfectly that the day of the Lord so cometh as a thief in the night.
> For when they shall say, Peace and safety; then sudden destruction cometh upon them, as travail upon a woman with child; and they shall not escape.
> But ye, brethren, are not in darkness, that that day should overtake you as a thief.
> Ye are all the children of light, and the children of the day: we are not of the night nor of darkness.
> Therefore let us not sleep, as do others; but let us watch and be sober (I Thess. 5:1-6).

The coming is the long promised Advent. Christ comes! He comes as an *avenger,* as a *judge,* as a *King,* as a *Bridegroom.* Like lightning, like a thief, like a snare. Like lightning to the world, but the Sun of morning to His Church; like a thief to the world, but like the cloud of glory to His own.

The Watching is not merely believing, nor hoping, nor waiting; but watching—as men do against some event, whether terrible or joyful, of which they know not the time.

Watch, for that day is great and glorious. Watch, for ye are naturally disposed to sit down and take your ease. Watch, for Satan tries to lull you to sleep. Watch, for the world with its wickedness and hatred, riches and vanities and pleasures, is trying to throw you off your guard. Be like Nehemiah the Hebrew devotee, a man of God and a patriot of prayer, who, when watching against the Ammonites, did not put off his clothes night and day. Keep your garments all about you, that when the Lord come He may not find you naked, but robed and ready. Blessed is that watcher; blessed is the keeper of his garments. Our Lord told his disciples that His Coming should fall "as a snare on all them that dwell on the face of the whole earth." But they are not to be surprised, but to be watching and ready.

When the happy hour of her wedding is fixed, long before the public is aware, the bride herself knows just when it is to take place, and indeed she has the most to say in fixing the date. It would be strange if the Bride of the Lamb of God should not at least know enough of the approaching of her Bridegroom to be robed and waiting. Indeed, the Lord's people have quite as much to do with the hastening of His Coming as the Lord Himself. To the late Dr. R. A. Torrey, distinguished scholar and Bible teacher, once a close associate to Dwight L. Moody, the honored teacher of this writer, who was impressing upon the minds of his thelogical students the above thought, I asked: "Do you mean to tell us, Dr. Torrey, that the soon and Second Coming of the Lord Jesus Christ is as much up to the people of God as it is to Him?"

"Precisely, Brother Krikorian," the world-renowned teacher replied. "That is exactly what I mean."

As Christians we are to fulfill the conditions and complete

the great preparation by clothing ourselves with garments of salvation and with the robe of righteousness as a bride adorneth herself with her jewels, which Christ Himself has prescribed.

> They that feared the LORD spake often to one another: and the LORD hearkened, and heard it, and a book of remembrance was written before him for them that feared the LORD, and that thought upon his name.
> And they shall be mine, saith the LORD of hosts, in that day when I make up my jewels; and I will spare them, as a man spareth his own son that serveth him (Mal. 3:16-17).

This, as Koestler said, is the "age of longing." Somehow we all feel that we are on the verge of a great happening, and there is worldwide a great expectancy. The brew of the centuries and the stew of time is stirring and is coming to a boil. This might indeed be the generation which sees fulfillment. Are we expectant? Are we ready?

IV

EVER-INTENSIFYING SIGNS OF
OUR SAVIOUR'S SECOND ADVENT

Christ's foretelling in His Olivet discourse of great calamities of world dimension, aroused in the disciples the question:

> Tell us, when shall these things be? and what shall be the sign of thy coming, and of the end of the world? (St. Matt. 24:3).
> And he said unto them, It is not for you to know the times or the seasons, which the Father hath put in his own power (Acts 1:7).

While therefore, God in His infinite wisdom has kept this secret, the course of the ages, to Himself, and we do not know the exact date, notwithstanding, the Word of God gives clear indications of world events that will precede His Coming, so that watchful believers, the children of the day, will not be overtaken as a thief if they are open to the signs of His appearing.

In dealing with the signs of the times and question of seasons associated with Christ's Second Coming, therefore, we must bear in mind that God does not measure time according to our calendars. The purposes of the Infinite are not scaled to the short measures of our hurry and flurry. We cannot imprison God on today's page of our engagement book. With Him, a thousand years are as one day, and one day as a thousand years. A single day often is fraught with issues as momentous as a whole century at other times. Spiritual conditions rather than mathematical figures measure God's great epochs. Let us then in the light of God's infallible Word reverently and in a quenchless faith trace some of the signs of the Son of man's Second Coming or acted parables of God's presence.

Natural Signs. The Lord Jesus Christ intimated repeatedly that there would be stupendous convulsions in the natural world when hills shall be removed, mountains would be overturned by the roots and rivers cut out among the rocks, preceding the Coming, and that earth and heaven would shake with the tread of His advance march.

> Nation shall rise against nation, and kingdom against kingdom:
> And great earthquakes shall be in divers places, and famines, and pestilences, and fearful sights and great signs shall there be from heaven (St. Luke 21:10-11).

Note carefully three clusters of phrases in this passage with their earthquakes, and fearful earth-shaking phenomena: "nation against nation." O spirit of mine, was there any period in human history when nations have been so against each other? A recent study of sixty centuries of human life and nations reveal that war has been more devastating and destructive of civilization in the first half of the twentieth century than in any other period of human history. "How and When the War may End in Vietnam" was the heavy headline in a popular magazine. The world had its Vietnam in southeast Asia with Hanoi and Saigon, Khe Sanh and Dien Bien Phu; Korea, North and South is in the same complicated conflict with a fresh war crisis at an opportune moment. Israel's "swift sword" and the Arab world in the Middle East; the emergent ex-colonial Africa, torn with brutal enmities, but travailing for the unattainable among the rapid transition and ideological struggle; Europe is in constant jitters of nuclear catastrophe; the Americas—Latin, South, North, experiencing fiery trials such as never seen before. The world of the twentieth century in inarticulate failure and frustration asks:

"What is the end that justifies wars of corruption and human slaughter where charnel and death casualties with 'garments rolled in blood,' have become the official measure of modern civilization?" Intangible wonder that Christ the victorious Messiah with dyed garments from Bozrah, glorious and marching in the greatness of His strenth, says: "I that . . . mighty to save" (Isaiah 63). In the meantime in His Olivet discourse He warns: "Ye shall hear of wars and rumours of wars; for all these things must come to pass" (St. Matt. 24:6).

Great Earthquakes. We know something of earthquakes— how they overturn and change the surfaces of countries, sink the hills, alter the courses of rivers, overwhelm vast populations, dry up lakes, set the mountains to vomiting fire, shake, toss, dart and agitate the mightiest seas in any part of the world. Earthquakes are fearful tremors that run through the whole frame of nature, filling the earth with consternation.

While this prophetic passage, "great earthquakes shall be in divers places," was under study as one of the earliest and intensifying signs of the imminent Coming of Christ, ten million Southern Californians experienced a shocking and disastrous earthquake of major proportion with scores dead, hundreds injured and property loss estimated in billions. Death and destruction were widespread, extending into the area until metropolitan Los Angeles felt the city was absorbing the ultimate in nuclear attack. A dozen highway overpasses collapsed and the celebrated Golden State Freeway buckled; gas mains ruptured and scores of raging fires burst into mighty flames meeting each other in fury and driving out 120,000 inhabitants from their homes. The quake was California's worst in nearly half a century that moved President Nixon to declare Southern California a major disaster area. There were those men and women in half-funeral; rescued from their terrifying tombs of dust and debris, who in the woeful words of a man who long ago experienced an earthquake testified: "I do fairly own that these earthquakes are very awful, and must be felt to be understood. Overwhelmed by some invisible power, beyond human control or comprehension, there comes the terrible sound; and immediately the solid earth is all in motion waving to and fro like the surface of the sea. Depend upon it, a severe earthquake is enough to shake the firmest mind. No one can witness it nor experience it without the deepest emotion of terror."

Authorities and geologists made no small contribution in building up tensions by warning the disaster-shocked and calamity-conditioned Californians with ringing alarms that in seismologically alive and quake-prone soil of the most populous state in the nation, earthquakes of catastrophic magnitude are inevitable. When Dr. Charles Francis Richter, professor emeritus of seismology at the prestigious California Institute of Technology was asked, "As a scientist, how would you describe the lesson that government officials might learn from this latest earthquake?", he answered poignantly: "No lesson could be learned from this earthquake." What these scientists and scholars of seismology seem to be suggesting is that scientists and savants of earthly wisdom cannot answer man's deepest questions and that such natural and fearsome phenomena still remain unanswered, because storms and earthquakes are natural symbols of divine wrath. The ancients regarded these terrifying disturbances as auguring and embodying the power and wrath of Deity. They are presented in the Scriptures and accordingly inwrought with all inspired diction as precursors and prophecies of the forthcoming judgment of God.

"Earthquakes and violent tremors in Chile," the land of the mighty Andes, writes an American Bible Society secretary, "are as common as breakfast eggs." Scarcely was the ink dry in these syllables on ivory surface, when news flashed over the radio that a shattering earthquake of exceptional violence had struck Northern Greece and Western Turkey, including Istanbul and the Dardanelles, causing much panic and loss of life in both countries and in the islands of the seas. To the

33

present time the total number of quakes and fearsome tremors in Turkey have reached more than 500. "Earthquake Kills in Japan and Stirs Tidal Waves," causing widespread damage, was the heavy headline in the public press. Hundreds of homes were flooded to the floor level and above. Roads became impassable, bridges and communication lines were cut, dikes ruptured and railway tracks severed. According to the Central Meteorological Agency, it was the strongest quake since the September 1, 1923 tremor that left much of Tokyo and Yokohama in ruins. What country and what part of this mortal sphere is immune to these ocean-shocking and earth-splitting seismic wonders and cosmic calamities beside which an atomic explosion would pale into insignificance—seismic wonders that bury living cities like "Herculaneum: Italy's buried treasure," for almost two thousand years; while turning up the lost Byzantine churches, and Crusaders' battlements come to view. How the Bible and these present phenomenal discoveries and grim ecological calamities fuse most strongly! The ground heaves and shakes and enormous lion-like roars come directly out of the bosom of the earth itself, as happened in the unbelievable six-hundred-mile devastation of Peru, leaving in its wake 40,000 dead, 150,000 injured and a million homeless. Associated with earthquakes, lightning and thunder, are the great floods such as the disastrous flood of Biblical dimension that struck Florence, the living city of the Renaissance of Italy in recent years.

The Friday, November 13, 1970 typhoon, in the densely populated region of the Ganges Delta at the top of the Bay of Bengal, East Pakistan, will go down in the annals of the world as one of the most shocking and horrifying disasters of the century. This, modern history's most disastrous natural catastrophe in its savage proportions, struck an area of 10,000 square miles wiping out 367,000 homes and a dozen islands with a population of more than five million, leaving, according to official information, 500,000 dead; and screaming and panicked millions tearing hungry and homeless in a horror of water and mud. Annual harvest being destroyed by overwhelmingly devastating storm, soaking the cut sheaves of rice and hurling them into a dike, survivors, half-crazed, with outstretched hands await help or death by widespread starvation and by the deadly epidemic and ever dangerous disease of Asiatic cholera.

A pilot who flew over the scene estimated as many as a million persons in a 10,000 square mile area may have been left homeless. He said there were no signs of life in some areas. Winds of the giant cyclone up to 150 miles an hour and 30-foot monstrous tidal waves that smashed Pakistan left in its wake thousands of floating bodies—too many to be disposed of; the corpses washed up like corks again and again with the tide on the black beaches of the Bay of Bengal—grim reminders of the great tragedy. Others were lifted and stuck in tree branches, while still more corpses were half buried in paddy fields and strewn in marshes—the grotesque evidence of human misery. Death was everywhere, with fearful loss of life in the greatest disaster from the sea in the history of the nation.

To hark back to the above question, what lesson can be learned from earthquakes, we must conclude that the sole and soul lesson governments and mankind universally could learn from these or any other earthquakes, storms and eclipses, are comprehended in Jesus Christ who knows the working of the natural universe. "For all things were created by him: and by him all things consist" (Col. 1:16-17). From him, "in whom are hid all the treasure of wisdom and knowledge" all men could learn the transcendent realities and mysteries that ever confront the human race. Christ, the absolute First Cause, in whom "dwelleth all the fulness of the God-head bodily" (Col. 2:9), invites: "Come learn of me." The prophet Isaiah proclaims

"Our God shall come, . . . the LORD of hosts with thunder, and with earthquake, and great noise, with storm

35

and tempest, and the flame of devouring fire . . . to shake the earth,"

Here is what Haggai, a minor prophet who majored in recording the sayings of the Lord of Hosts says:

"Yet once, ... and I will shake the heavens, and the earth, and the sea, and the dry *land;* And I will shake all nations."

The full force of this earthquake, unprecedented in time for its extent and violence is indicated in its effects when the Holy City broke into three parts and the cities of the nations fell.

The earthquakes that attended the Crucifixion and Resurrection of Christ are not only the signs of His Second Coming, but the greatest earthquake will take place when "the Lord cometh down, and tread upon the high places of the earth and the mountains shall be molten under his feet:" chiefly the Mount of Olives which is before Jerusalem. The mountain shall cleave in the midst from east to west through the mightiest earthquake this planet has ever experienced, the shock and impact of which will be felt around the world; creating new rivers, new islands, new atmospheric changes in the heavens, new mountains. New and great valleys shall be cleft as wax before the fire.

But who shall abide the day of his coming? and who shall stand when he appeareth? for he is like a refiner's fire (Mal. 3:2).

To this cry of the soul, the ageless answer and redemptive response is: "He that hath clean hands and a pure heart." Only those who can find the real transcendence in the discovery of reality of God in Christ can live creatively, faithfully and in an assured hope of his appearing.

In an age of cosmic chaos therefore, the earthquakes have

their message to deliver and lesson to teach! That message, that lesson with ultimate appropriateness and divine fitness is the imminent Coming of the Lord Jesus Christ to establish his Kingdom of righteousness and peace on earth.

Fearful Sights. Who has not read about that fearful sight, an awesome night view as molten lava flowed from the fiery volcanic cone to the icy waters of the shocked North Atlantic in black columns of eruption off the coast of Iceland in 1963? Amid awesome explosions, the sea in great pangs gave birth to a son in the form of an island with noble dimensions of 567 feet in height and more than one square mile in area. This grandiose performance and the thunderous symphony of the elements, spewed out of a submarine volcanic eruption catapulting incandescent lava bombs, is a miracle of creation. These are acts of God embodying a purpose of eternal quality and fulfillment of a prophecy by the Great Apostle Peter who, looking into the depths of his time, saw a sign definitely connected with Christ's Second Coming and certainty of the end.

> But the day of the Lord will come as a thief in the night; in the which the heavens shall pass away with a great noise, and the elements shall melt with fervent heat, the earth also and the works that are therein shall be burned up (II Peter 3:10).

Political Sign. The Lord Jesus Christ announced that the end should be marked by terrific wars, military armaments and great distress in the social and political world; Conflicts between labor and capital.

> And ye shall hear of wars and rumors of wars: see that ye be not troubled: for all these things must come to pass, but the end is not yet.
> For nation shall rise against nation, and kingdom against kingdom: and there shall be famines, and pestilences, and earthquakes, in divers places (St. Matt. 24:6-7).
> But when ye shall hear of wars and commotions, be not

terrified: For these things must first come to pass; but the end is not by and by (St. Luke 21:9).

The nations with all their creative genius, exciting discoveries and phenomenal conquest of planetary space have only succeeded in building about themselves a turbulent and anxious world, the dominant notes of which are conflict and violence. Since the dawn of history, no less than forty civilizations have come and gone. Old nations have crumbled and new ones arisen with higher culture; yet the posterity of the most brilliant civilizations are plunged back into the same abyss of barbarism over which their own enlightened and immediate ancestors apparently had triumphed. Novicow, a very painstaking student of history poignantly has stated that: From the year 1496 B.C. to 1861 A.D., in 3,357 years, there were 227 years of peace and 3,310 years of war. . . . From the year 15 B.C. to 1860 A.D., more than 8000 treaties of peace, meant to remain in force forever, were concluded. The average time they remained in force is two years. "I have been forced to the conclusion," says Charles A. Lindbergh, "that an overemphasis on science weakens human character and upsets life's essential balance. Science breeds technology. Technology leads to infinite complication. Examples are everywhere: in the intricacy of government and of business corporations; in automation and labor relations; in war, diplomacy, legislation, taxation, in almost every field of modern man's routine. If we are to escape," continues this man of original mind, "the catastrophes that have ended earlier civilizations, we must learn that man cannot live by science and intellect alone."

Now that we are on the eschatological subject, it is an accepted understanding by all Bible scholars and prophetic students that the Imperial Head of Caesar's original Roman Empire representing the ten kingdomed confederacy, prefigured by the ten-horned beast of Daniel (7:7; Rev. 13) embracing the ten leading European nations, viz., Britain, separated legislatively from Ireland; France extended to the Rhine, Belgium, Luxembourg, Switzerland the Rhine province; Spain with Portugal; Italy; Austria; Greece with Macedonia, Albania, Thessaly, Epirus; Egypt; Syria; Thracian Turkey; Danubian States; are to be restored. The momentous decision of England after a ten-year bid to join the European Common Market membership of nations— France, West Germany, Italy, Belgium, the Netherlands and Luxembourg, on January 1, 1973, upon the clearing of imposing hurdles and highly charged issues all along the way, might well be the beginning of the revival of the Roman Empire, indicating that Christ's Coming is near. This astounding geographical and revolutionary change of the countries chiefly around the Mediterranean Sea is to prepare the way for the Antichrist's brief span and frightful reign, and the world is rapidly preparing itself for an unprecedented dictatorship under his imperial rule. The greater portion of the world population has been oriented to democracy; but democracy itself has been uncertainly eroding. If the world's democratic system is to work effectively, there must be respect for divinely ordained authority. "For," says the Apostle Paul, one of the greatest logicians and legal minds in all the ages of the Church; "the governments are ordained of God" (Rom. 13:1). Respect for laws of the land, then, is based upon the fundamental law of God and voluntary obedience to His clearly defined will and purpose. But when any society turns its back upon God and His Word and follows the devices of its heart and choosing, as in mid-twentieth century America, then the handwriting of any democratic system is on the wall: "Te kel Upharsin"—"Thou art weighed in the balances, and art found wanting" (Daniel 5:27).

Dictators are appearing in every continent, and the world slowly but surely is heading for unusual dictatorship and Antichrist, a figure belonging to the last hour. Some years ago, while a theological student, this author listened on a Sunday afternoon to a brilliant minister of the Gospel. The preacher in addressing that distinguished gathering, took fire, rose higher and in the masterly pulpiteering for which he was noted, delivered an eloquent and impassioned oration in which he dramatically portrayed Kaiser Wilhelm of Hohenzollern fame of World War I as the Antichrist. Adolph Hitler, who urged a destiny for world leadership for Nazi Germany, and his lesser collaborator Benito Mussolini, as well as Joseph Stalin of Soviet Russia were also spoken of as antichrists during World War II. While these warrior dictators of violence and blood, who for a brief span ruled as if they were gods of the cosmos, displayed thereby some aspects of "the Man of Sin," their collapse of time and awkward spread in death stand as a poignant footnote to history. All their advocates therefore, profane or religious, had to admit that in them they were wrong.

On May 7, the year of our Lord 1834, alluding to the immense British Empire on which the "sun never set," Daniel Webster in his characteristic eloquence said: "A power which has dotted over the surface of the whole globe with her possessions and military posts, whose morning drumbeat following the sun, and keeping company with the hours, circles the earth with one continuous and unbroken strain of the martial airs of England." How differently the bold black headline in a mid-twentieth century magazine reads: "Britain's Decline and Fall," 134 years later. A haunting cartoon depicts John Bull, the Englishman personified, looking to his right toward the distant horizon to the sun half set; and while wiping his tears he speaks the melting words of valediction and parting salutation: "FAREWELL TO ALL MY GREATNESS!"

So a great empire once so immense as to cover this mortal sphere, on which the sun never set, is lost—gone; and Churchill's England of which he said: "There shall always be one," painfully seeks to adjust her destiny to a role of minor power in today's stern and strange world. No more significant and startling political event can be imagined as a sign of

Christ's Second Coming before our very eyes than this dramatic development in the life of once so dynamic a nation.

This significant political event and the liquidation of great empires includes other great empires also; the Great German Empire; Austro-Hungarian Empire; French Empire; Belgian Empire; Dutch Empire and Ottoman Empire. Their disappearance is a sobering sign of the Second Coming of Christ: the rightful King of God's Kingdom.

Commercial Sign. When prophet Daniel, "a man greatly beloved," asked some particular signs of the winding up of time, the Angel as his last message to God's honored man answered: "Many shall run to and fro." Not only on land and sea, but the very air and stratosphere are shaken with the ear-splitting thunder and roar of airplanes, commercial jets, comets, rockets and other armadas; creatures of increased wisdom and phenomenal knowledge. To again quote Charles A. Lindbergh: "Supersonic transports will carry passengers at rifle-bullet speed. Spaceships are planned for traveling between earth, moon and nearby planets. The study of nucleonics places cosmic power in our hands, while cryobiology may suspend the human aging process. We dream of hurtling through galaxies as did our ancestors of imitating birds. Obviously the developmental potential in all scientific fields is tremendous, extending far beyond our vision." Modern man is leaving nothing unturned to build a tower to reach the moon and stars and heaven. He, seeking to fulfill the Arch Tempter's first promise to Adam in Paradise: "Ye shall be as gods." An eminent author has said that the nineteenth century advanced human progress more than all the centuries before and that the first decade of the twentieth century has surpassed the whole of the nineteenth century. What would have been the eloquent rhetoric of the good appraiser of time, had he been asked to estimate the twentieth century to its half and more? Surely God, the Creator, is giving to His people in these unprecedented days of miraculous communication and knowledge media the signs of a larger and final emancipation of all the universe; the signs of and earnest of the coming age by the return of Jesus Christ.

The Moral Sign. This is one of God's table of contents for the last page of human history:

> The wicked shall do wickedly: and none of the wicked shall understand (Daniel 12:10).
> Evil men and seducers shall wax worse and worse, deceiving and being deceived (II Tim. 3:13).

How prophetic these scriptural passages sound for our times of social strife, outbreak of violence, racial ferment and explosion, urban anarchy, riots, armed insurrection, arrogant flouting and the defiance of law and order, in a paroxysm of terror assault on the nation's institutions, including the Church and schools by the disciples of death and destruction; a pestilence and national and international agony seldom surpassed in the history of America: a rebellion that verges on treason.

And what of the drug-oriented hippie movement; a potentially destructive philosophy of faithless retreat; an attitude and form of escapism from moral integrity and personal responsibility and pure reality that has become a "copout"; a hideaway from society. These neurotic groups, a bizarre subculture with its deluded dropouts, avid for sensations and childish fascination, roll their marijuana, the hallucinogenic weed, into cigarettes, ignite them, puff them and in their psychedelic paranoia, self-indulgence and inner restlessness are off to clouds somewhere in the stratosphere; lost to themselves and lost to God. How fitting here is the admonition of Paul, the Master Apostle, "Redeem the time, because the days are evil." He, perhaps next to his Lord and Master the most influential personality in religious history, by making Christianity the universal religion of the world in foretelling of the wickedness and apostasy of the last days, describes indeed the moral decadence of the twentieth century.

This know also, that in the last days perilous times shall come.

For men shall be lovers of their own selves, covetous, boasters, proud, blasphemers, disobedient to parents, unthankful, unholy,

Without natural affection, truce-breakers, false accusers, incontinent, fierce, despisers of those that are good,

Traitors, heady, highminded, lovers of pleasures more than lovers of God; (II Tim. 3:1-4).

A high government official who has been characterized as the "calmest man in the capital" of the nation says: "the moral order is not something static, it is not something enshrined in historic documents, or lodged in the minds of pious moralists. It is an attribute of a functioning moral system. As such, it is a changing, living thing liable to decay and disintegration as well as to revitalization and reinforcement."

In a day of independence from and disbelief in God Almighty, the attempt to outlaw the Bible for the administration of oaths, the removal from the national coins: "In God We Trust," to delete "Under God" from the Pledge of Allegiance, and firm reliance on the protection of "Divine Providence" from the Thanksgiving Day Presidential Proclamation as well as days of Prayer; ah, these are signs indeed of moral decay that portend the Coming of Christ.

At the dawn of creation, the first man rebelled against the law and rule of God. Since then, men have rebelled against the rule of man. Everywhere we are witnessing a growing disrespect for law and order. And the startling thing we are witnessing today is that the court and crowd often side with evil-doers against officers of the law. "They that forsake the law praise the wicked" (Prov. 28:4). The nearer we get to the end of human world history by the Coming of Christ, the more acute become the symptoms! "Evil men and seducers shall wax worse and worse, deceiving and being deceived" (II Tim. 3:13).

No less an authority than the late J. Edgar Hoover, director of the Federal Bureau of Investigation, writing in the current issue of the "FBI Law Enforcement Bulletin" said: "The publication and sale of obscene material is *BIG* business in America today. Degenerate sex pictures and pornographic literature, covertly peddled and sold in most cities and communities, net greedy smut merchants millions of dollars annually. It is impossible to estimate the amount of harm to impressionable teen-agers and to assess the volume of sex crimes attributable to pornography, but its influence is alarmingly extensive. Many parents are deeply concerned."

Is our society becoming so wicked that we are turning from virtue and integrity to immorality and degradation? Are we becoming morally bankrupt and letting our principles of conduct and decency deteriorate? Are we forsaking the simple teachings of right over wrong and good over bad?

Let us look about us. In the publishing, theatrical and entertainment fields, are the good, enlightening and educational qualities of their products being overshadowed by too much emphasis on obscenity and vulgarity?

Many people believe this to be true. But the legitimate productions of these media are rather mild when compared with the hard-core pornography flooding the country in the form of film, playing cards, comic books, paperbacks and pictures.

Such filth in the hands of young people and curious adolescents does untold damage and leads to disastrous consequences. The Saviour Himself, particularly and frequently, admonished His college of disciples that the gigantic iniquities and sensualities of Noah's and Lot's days, would repeat themselves as the end approaches, and that the judgments of the great day would be preeminently deserved by the generation then living. The late Dr. Thomas S. Gates, for many years president of the University of Pennsylvania, in his last statement, posthumously released, appealed: "If our civilization dries up or is destroyed, it will be because the sources of moral conduct have dried up, at the precise time when moral problems are most pressing." He advocated religion "in no watered down version" be made a requirement in the educational preparation of every college student. "It is a step which demands that we be bold rather than cautious," he wrote. In bold letters the distinguished educator pointedly emphasized: *"Our Education has failed to Give Moral Guidance to World's Leaders."* Dr. Gates continued: "Knowledge and skills have been perfected. Universities present and teach the sciences, the languages, the arts, the philosophies, but conspicuously do not offer religion. We must learn that religion takes over where science leaves off." Intangible wonder that Carl Gustav Jung—the last survivor of psychologists' Big Three declared: "The central neurosis of our time is emptiness."

Ecclesiastical Sign. Consider conditions in the Christian Church today, which the Lord said should mark the time of the end. We see confusion and disarray; a sounding of uncertain trumpets; a "falling away," a departure from the faith, which was delivered unto the saints; a rejection of the "common Salvation" and removal of the landmarks that once separated the Church and people of God from the world. The spirit of lying liberalism and the stunning spectacle of antichristian infidelity that manifests itself in daring avowals of abominable atheism denies the reality of a creative Deity and the existence of an omnipotent God in modern life and civilization. And this is done not only by arrogant and ignorant secularists, but by aggressively speculative professors and theologians who are supported by the ecclesiastical bodies of the day. When in the absence of spiritual commitment, denial of faith and secularism becomes a religion, where love of God and blessed hope in Christ in the Church appears to be not only on the wane, but withering and dying; are not these the fulfillment of our Lord's solemn prophecy: "When the Son of man cometh shall he find faith on earth"?

The Church is the assembly of God's called and chosen

45

people, manifest in the fellowship and profession of the rights and signs of revealed Christianity. Obviously, however, this assembly is composed of more than one class of people: the class of the truly regenerate, whom God has begotten as His own children, and in whom the Church has its life—characterized as the congregation of saints; but along with them another class, nominal outward members, who in living reality have not yet attained to the rank of God's children. It is quite evident to those who look, that not all are saints who profess Christianity and observe its rites; but who are the true members are known to God only. The Church, then, is a sowing of God on earth and the planting of Jesus Christ; but it has been oversown by the enemy and the wicked one. The Creator sowed some good seed in Paradise; but when it came to the harvest, the principal product was tares—darnels of the devil. At earth's first altar appeared the slayer with the saint—Cain with Abel. The Almighty had His sons before the great flood; but the children of the evil one outnumbered them all. Since then and in all ages and dispensations, the plants of grace have ever found the weeds springing up by their sides, their roots intertwining, and their stalks and leaves and fruits putting forth together. The Church itself has never been an exception, and never will be until the Lord of the harvest at His Second Coming orders His reapers to separate the tares from the wheat. Incredible as it may sound, the Church even in its first and purest periods was intermixed with Antichrists: Judas among its apostles; Ananias and Simon Magus among its first converts; Demas and Diatrephes among public servants and its men of sin in the temple of God.

When we consider the corruption, deterioration, and ever-increasing apostasy of the present Church; when we read in the Holy Scriptures that in the last days the form of godliness shall be found lingering over the utmost excesses of unrighteousness; the pure truth of God be no longer tolerated by professed Christendom in its eagerness for religious novelties and sensations; and "faith of our fathers" has almost vanished from the earth; when we contemplate the prophetic pictures of the consummate paganism and perversion of everything sacred and true which is to mark the closing periods of this dispensation; there is no room for wonder at the final command to cast out the unclean things. It is the eternal law of things, that unfaithfulness invites judgment, that if the Church apostasizes, it dissolves just as any other cult and religious sect.

What does it all mean? It seems that the Church, as a professing body, pure and excellent as it was in the beginning, and with all the partial and periodic revivals that mark its career, and with all the cloud and company of saints it has embraced, is yet, in the judgment of the Son of God Himself, a subject of ever-increasing decline and decay, first in one direction, then in another, until the full-scale heresy and apostasy sets her in danger of rejection. This strikes the death-knell to the humanitarian doctrine of temporal Millennium, and to the hopes of an ecclesiastical renewal of the world.

It is the Church of the Laodicean age: lukewarm, uncertain, partly hot partly cold, divided between Christ and the world, not willing to surrender pretensions and claims to the heavenly, and yet clinging close to the earthly, having too much conscience to cast off the name of Christ, and too much love for the world to take a firm and honest stand wholly on His side. To such "the faithful and true Witness" hath given His word: "I am about to spew you out of my mouth."

We are in the midst of such days right now. At a meeting of the National Council of Churches, as reported by the magazine *Christianity Today,* one-third of the delegates could not affirm their faith in the reality of God! More than one-third could not subscribe to the Deity of Jesus Christ! Two-thirds did not believe in miracles! The Council also went on record as holding "love of neighbor" to be more important for salvation than personal "belief in Jesus Christ as Saviour"!

There is again an increasing and revolutionary tendency in the land by neo-modernists, watered down liberalists and assorted Erasmusian humanists, to take the best of the world's great religions and make of them one great homogenized faith (syncretism) and to look upon all types of religious faiths as being of equal importance and containing equal truth (latitudinarianism), which threatens to invade the Church and enervate her evangelistic concern and depth of passion, ending in an inner collapse.

In this awful and awkward age, when violent voices of doubt and disbelief tear and taunt, when militant atheism and materialistic totalitarianism in vociferous and derisive challenges are threatening the Christian way of life, and *selling out God Himself—the supreme issue of history;* we, the custodians of a spiritual evangel, need a heightened and dynamic Christian experience in our battle for the Lord, if "His truth is to triumph through us." This is the valid appeal and vigorous aim of this interpretation at this critical eleventh hour which calls for a maximum Christian experience of highest distinction between what we are and what we are capable of becoming; between life's downward drag and the pull of the stars of God which beckon us heavenward.

In our day, much of what we call Christian experience is only a dialect compared with the first-century Church which, amid life's strain and stress, in quest of a higher voltage of spiritual experience and completed Christian personality, treasured Jesus Christ for a lifetime and attained to "a splendor greater yet while serving Him."

The Church of the newborn, free from heresy, indeed lives in a world of bewildering problems. Made of flesh and blood, at the same time human and divine, her God-ordained function, as described in a second-century document called the "Letter of Diognetus": in spite of all denials and general falling away, is "to penetrate all ranks of society, involve herself deeper in racial and social concerns, giving a spiritual tone and substance to every living thing." President Nixon, in

48

addressing eighty religious leaders and Church officials of most of the nation's major denominations on the spreading drug abuse that is alarming the American people, said: "It is a spiritual problem and a spiritual need. If there is an answer you have it. Drug abuse causing not only physical but psychic damage, society loses its sense of spiritual values upon which all else must rest." In a day-long program to orient churchmen about multifaceted approaches by government, the president charged and challenged the members of the religious group in a White House session, reminding them, "you know what enormous responsibility you have in this area."

How different is the mid-twentieth century finding of the American Institute of Public Opinion from that of the second century Diognetic document: "that Churches should not speak out on political and social problems and issues of the day." The Church's mission is not only to raise the religious level and practice of the people, but it is her moral and spiritual obligation also to take a stand like the prophets of old and speak with the moral insight of the Gospel against evil and wrong and issues of life in the contemporary world; for Christianity pervades all life—all of life as demonstrated by Christ Himself. There is an unmistakable concern in Jesus' moral teachings. He condemned as hypocrites the scribes and Pharisees who ostentatiously tithed their possessions but neglected the "weightier matters of the law, judgment, mercy and faith" (St. Matt. 23:23).

A perceptive observer said recently that a great many Americans who are essentially kind and decent folk seem to be suffering from "compassion fatigue." Webster defines compassion as "sympathetic consciousness of others' distress, together with a desire to alleviate it." If you feel sorry for a person in need, that's pity. If you care enough about his troubles to try to help, that's compassion. All Biblicists are familiar with the apostolic admonition to the Church in Galatia centuries ago: "Let us not be weary in well doing": do not become tired of doing good. This could be fittingly addressed to the contemporary Church of all faiths. For as the soul to the body, so are truly born again Christians to the world. What this means in essence is that a commitment to love others cannot be separated from faith in Christ, who having Himself made His commitment to God, demanded that same commitment. In Churchillian rhetoric, this era of ecumenical breakthrough, doctrinal pluralism and sectarian particularities of belief, O Church of the redeemed, possessor of the sanctifying grace of God calling for bloody and sweaty goodness achieved by fallible men and women, is thy finest hour. The fallible men and women, who in the soul-making process like the Son of Man in dark Gethsemane, by noblest and responsible choice, meet and master the world while looking for His Coming. This is a fundamental premise of future-oriented faith. The Church, in the Biblical perspective, is the vanguard of the Kingdom, the eschatological community whose transcendent life is to serve as the sign within this secular society with the hope of a Messianic age.

Bishop John T. Robinson of England, the author of the controversial book *Honest to God,* during a visit to the United States, delivered at a seminar of fifty-five American and European theologians and scholars, the funeral oration of the Church, saying that he "looks forward to the death of the Church and welcomes it." It is our understanding that by the death of the Church, the eminent ecclesiastic meant the death of denominational organizations which are essentially committed to the status quo; sectarianism with which the field has been littered; highly visible and rigid institutions tied down with canonical knots; static and monumental hierarchies and imposing earth-oriented edifices which are like the outer shells and vestures of the sower's grain of wheat destined to disintegrate to promote new life, please God—hundredfold. To this vision of spiritual emancipation of the Church and her recovery of the inward glow of God's "good fire," the continued flourishing of spiritual vitality; we fain would add our "Amen!" And to our Amen we would give full measure of devotion to the end that the universal body of Christ, searching for the shores of a new life, rededicate herself in a full-orbed and vital renewal and all-out commitment to the servanthood; "the food of sound faith" in the midst of the world's pockets of poverty and social concern which was the urgent aim and consuming passion of Him who declared the true image of the living Church: "I am among you as he that serveth."

> The Church—the Church—the holy Church—
> The Saviour's spotless Bride!
> Who does not love her queenly form
> Above all earth beside!
> Be ours through life to live in her;
> And when the Lord of life shall call,
> To die in her, the spouse of Christ,
> The mother of one and of us all.

Spiritual Signs. Dreary as the annals of the Church appear, both in prophetic and historic records, the student of them still finds his path skirted with spiritual verdure; and in the distant scenery, examples of faith, purity, love, heroism, devotion and obedience are never once entirely out of view; the loveliest often being found in the bypaths, and encountered where they would be least expected. Even in the darkest eras imbedded in neglected chronicles, noble names are to be found, sparkling with the radiance of every Christian grace. And so, in all the ages, there have never failed some blessed offsets to the ever downward tendency of things. Nor will it ever be, in the darkest and most dread days of Christendom's apostasy, that there will be none to stand up for God and His pure truth, or that His true people shall fail from the earth.

The prophet Daniel, who in his last message received from the angel the moral sign, in the same verse gives us the spiritual signs. "Many shall be purified and made white, and tried; but the wicked shall do wickedly" (Dan. 12:10). We read

51

in the prophetic message to Dumah, that anxious Edomite, unable to sleep, oppressed by a strange feeling that something ominous is going to happen, turns into the dark, silent and deserted street. Hearing the heavy footfall of the watchman pacing back and forth on the city walls, he cries out: "Watchman, what of the night?" (Isaiah 21:11). When will the day dawn?

This Old Testament narrative awakens within me a haunting memory of more than three score years which I experienced in my early teens in the Bible lands. Caught in the throes of shivering chill and consuming fever, unable to sleep at night, in desperation and semi-delirium, I called repeatedly, "Ana, Sabah oldoumou?" Mother, is it the morning? How near is the daybreak? Softly and tenderly she would whisper the prayerful words of assurance; "Patience, my son, patience. Another day of our Father-God is approaching."

The man of Seir, like myself, was in earnest; he calls again and again: "Watchman, what of the night? Watchman, what of the night?" When will the day dawn? The watchman answered, "The morning cometh"; morning fresh and clear, dewy and delightful, bracing and beautiful, a morning of joy and prosperity. So is the historical application of this holy oracle in the life of the Church and the world. Every true-hearted, earnest Christian and apocalyptic believer, as I longed for the dawn of the day, longs for the advent of the world's new morning, when the dark shadows shall flee and the pitchy mantle of night of unbelief, irreligion and materialistic atheism shall be driven away by the streaks of a sunny dawn and by the increasing life of faith and holiness.

> If I say, surely the darkness shall cover me; even the night shall be light about me (Ps. 139:11).

There will be an outpouring of the blessed Holy Spirit as "the latter rain," upon a ripening harvest field, upon those who are willing to walk with God, like Enoch, in holy obedience. So, many shall be purified and made white. It is the wedding garment of the Bride, purged through trials and finally crowned at His coming with victory and honor through Him who overcame the world.

> The righteous shall flourish like the palm tree: he shall grow like a cedar in Lebanon.
> Those that be planted in the house of the Lord shall flourish in the courts of our God (Ps. 92:12-13).

Lighted by the light of the Lord that beats upon the great white throne, and like a rainbow in full-orbed glory, spanning the gap from earth to heaven, the righteous shall flourish like the palm tree and grow like the cathedrallike cedars of Lebanon. From a great depth of spiritual being nourished by the living and creative power of the omnipotent God, supreme carver of the universe, who made us souls as well as the swinging stars in glory; spiritually sensitive and seasoned saints shall adorn the courts of God. Heaven and earth, this wandering planet spinning in the whirlpool of space, with its deafening roar of human traffic and the thunder of global contentions, might be shaken by storm clouds, black with muttering wrath, but Christ's own, the great body and bride spiritual, the visible Kingdom of God on this mortal sphere, "striving against sin" with majestic faith, cannot be moved.

A secular commentator sums up his philosophy thus: "We have come through the pagan 20's, the depressing 30's, the warring 40's, the A-bomb 50's, and on into the nuclear 60's." Armored with the divine assurance above, the righteous becomes a spiritual force and a conquering power, yes, even in a nuclear age. By redemptively reaffirming his faith and love, with fewer words but much more heart, the godly, like the first despised minority that changed the history of the world, glories with great rapture in the widening horizons, looking for that long range and blessed hope and the glorious appearing of the great God, and our Saviour Jesus Christ.

In the fourteenth verse of the twenty-fourth chapter of the Gospel according to Saint Matthew, embracing the famed Olivet discourse, comprehensive of eschatological events of cosmic dimension, we have one of the greatest signs of the imminent return of the Lord Jesus Christ. To the threefold question of his disciples, "When shall these things be? what shall be the sign of thy coming; and of the end of the world?" He answered, "This Gospel of the Kingdom shall be preached in all the world for a witness unto all nations; and then shall the end come."

Never since these prophetic phrases fell upon the quickened spirits of His college of disciples on the Mount of Olives have there been so many amazing avenues for worldwide Gospel preaching. Like the spiritual phenomena on the Day of Pentecost, all peoples hear the Gospel of the Kingdom in their own tongues. Never before has it been possible to present the name of Jesus Christ as the Saviour of the world to all of the human race as it is today. Of this age it can be verily said: "The earth is full with the knowledge of the Lord, as the waters cover the sea." Surely of this age it cannot be said there is "a famine of the hearing of the words of the Lord": for it is now possible not only to hear the preacher of the Gospel all over the world through the miracle of radio but to see him through the marvel of television—a revolution and revival indeed in mass communication, through transmitters in the sky, through wide-screen multimedia presentations of films and greatly accelerated testimonies.

"I hope we shall never forget that we created this nation," said Woodrow Wilson, "not to serve ourselves, but to serve mankind." "Go ye into all the world, and preach the Gospel to every creature" was the great commission of Him, who had created and trained a band of disciples and who said to them, "I am among you as he that serveth." On that day the Church militant in obedience to the divine assignment caught the vision of a worldwide proclamation of the Gospel and kept it unto the present. Christians in their on-going ministry and sacrificial service went to Asia's teeming millions, to the great continent of Africa, to Hispanic America overshadowed by the semidarkness of an authoritarian hierarchy; and to the Islands of the Seven Seas. Europe too, in spite of its galaxy of religious reformers, consultative bodies, formally structured organizations of professional and religious teachers, needed the articulate power of the pure and efficacious voice of the Gospel to liberate her from the prevailing agnosticism and destructive criticism which mocked religion and profaned the doctrine of Christianity.

The great inventions of radio and television already mentioned, and breath-taking speed of modern jets and transport ships and planes that convey preachers, teachers, evangelists and missionaries to the uttermost part of the earth in short hours are preparing the way for Christ's Second Coming as John the Baptist prepared the way for His First Coming. In his message the intrepid evangel recalls the prophecy of the promulgation of the Gospel of Isaiah fame.

> Prepare ye the way of the LORD, make straight in the desert a highway for our God.
> Every valley shall be exalted, and every mountain and hill shall be made low: and the crooked shall be made straight, and the rough places plain.
> And the glory of the LORD shall be revealed, and all flesh shall see it together; for the mouth of the LORD hath spoken it (Isaiah 40:3-5).

This unprecedented preparation for the final proclamation of the Gospel "for a witness unto all the nations" points to "the end" at Christ's Second Coming. The Holy Bible itself, now being printed in nearly 100 languages is a significant fulfillment of the great hymn of Charles Wesley fame: "O for a thousand tongues to sing my great redeemer's praise." Intangible wonder that the prophet of Patmos and revelator, seeing in an apocalyptic vision this very age, wrote:

I saw another angel fly in the midst of heaven, having the everlasting gospel to preach unto them that dwell on the earth, and to every nation, and kindred, and tongue and people.

Saying with a loud voice, Fear God, and give glory to him; for the hour of his judgment is come: and worship him that made heaven, and earth, and the sea, and the fountains of waters (Rev. 14:6, 7).

I looked, and behold a white cloud, and upon the cloud one sat like unto the Son of man, having on his head a golden crown, and in his hand a sharp sickle (Rev. 14:14).

What a great sign, this final preaching of the Gospel to every nation, and kindred and tongue and people in this climactic hour in the history of this mortal sphere just before the return of the Lord Jesus Christ, adorned on His head with a golden and imperial crown and in His hand a sharp sickle comprehensive of the harvest which is the end of the world.

Jewish Sign. Of the six and ever-intensifying scriptural signs: natural, political, commercial, moral, ecclesiastical and spiritual, each representing a particular relevance to the apocalypse of Jesus Christ and His Second Advent "with power and great glory," we now come undoubtedly to the most important, namely, the Sign of Israel.

Speaking to his congregation some years ago, an English divine said: "My people, there is a land which is unlike any other land on this earth. That land is Palestine. There is a people unlike any other people created by God. That people is Israel. And there is a book unlike any other book written by man. That book is the Judaeo-Christian Holy Book: the Bible. The only place where you will find any authoritative information about either the people or the land is in that book."

As we proceed with our study of this sign "unlike" any other sign, let us bear in mind the above three areas of thought: the Book, the people of Israel and the land. The Book unlike any other book, the Holy Bible, the only source of authoritative information, defines and illustrates the real boundaries of God's Palestine. The following passages of the Holy Scripture embracing the Abrahamic Covenant read:

> In the same day the Lord made a covenent with Abram, saying, Unto thy seed have I given this land, from the river of Egypt unto the great river, the river Euphrates (Gen. 15:18).

God added to the Abrahamic Covenent the Sinaitic Covenant, saying:

> I will set your bounds from the Red Sea to the sea of the Philistines [the Mediterranean], and from the wilderness to the river [Euphrates]; for I will deliver the inhabitants of the land into your hand, and you shall drive them out before you (Exodus 23:31).
> Thou art the Lord the God, who didst choose Abram, and broughtest him forth out of Ur of the Chaldees, and gavest him the name of Abraham,
> And foundest his heart faithful before thee, and madest a covenant with him to give the land of the Canaanites, the Hittites, the Amorites and the Perizzites, and the Jebusites, and the Girgashites, to give it, I say, to his seed, and hast performed thy words; for thou art righteous; (Neh. 9:7-8).

Now as we square off these boundaries of the Abrahamic covenant, from the Nile on the south to the Euphrates on the north; from the Arabian desert on the east to the Mediterranean on the west; we will find a land area nearly twenty-five times the size of modern Palestine. And it is a scientifically known fact that the land is rich in oil, chemicals, raw materials, precious metals and most productive "sacred soil." When the momentous news of the first oil strike in the history of Israel was flashed over the young nation's radio, it was prefaced with the reading of a Biblical passage from Deuteronomy 32:13 telling how the Lord brought Jacob out of the wilderness into a land where he could "suck . . . oil out of the flinty rock." Prospectors have discovered oil, copper and other riches in Israel—right where the Scriptures said they were! It contains more than two-thirds of the known oil resources in the world today, over and above the multibillion dollar wealth of chemicals in the Dead Sea; a rich prize indeed, that someday will cost Russia her national existence; "but the sixth part." The exciting and historic drive of modern Russia toward the warm waters of the great Mediterranean to convert it into a Soviet lake and Russian Mare Nostrum by arming and bolstering with latest missiles her tottering client, Egypt, to the X-ray eyes of the world will inevitably hasten and ultimately seal her doom. The renowned day of Russia will be her burial in Israel (Ez. 39:2, 11-13).

No modern nation is set forth so vividly in the prophetic Word as is Russia. Probably the reason is that the Eternal, looking down across the sands of time, beheld Russia, as no other nation, raising her mighty fists and hissing her defiance. It is recalled that Stalin of Russia signed the official decree in 1932 ordering the Almighty to pack His few belongings and get out of the Soviet empire. That decree, according to the London *Morning Post,* read:

On May 1, 1937, there must not remain on the territory of the U.S.S.R. a single house of prayer to God, and the very conception "God" will be banished from the boundaries of the Soviet Union, as a survival of the Middle Ages which has served as an instrument for the oppression of the working masses.

The date is past. We have not as yet heard that the Almighty took His exit.

Once again the authoritative information recorded in the Bible of the Abrahamic Covenant, confirmed and made everlasting by El Shaddai, Almighty God, is that by divine election and promise, Israel owns the land. To the contentious question and counterclaims of Israeli and Arab, "whose land is Palestine?" the irrefutable answer is, Israel's!

> And I will give unto thee, and to thy seed after thee, the land wherein thou art a stranger, all the land of Canaan, for an everlasting possession; and I will be their God (Gen. 17:8).

And lest any should lay claim to this promise "thy seed," for Ishmael's descendants, and that is being done today by many Arab sympathizers, God makes it very clear which seed is to inherit the land.

> And God said, Sarah thy wife shall bear thee a son indeed: and thou shalt call his name Isaac: and I will establish my covenant with him for an everlasting covenant, and with his seed after him (Gen. 17:19).
>
> The earth is the LORD'S, and the fulness thereof; the world and they that dwell therein (Ps. 24:1).
>
> I know that, whatsoever God doeth, it shall be forever: nothing can be put to it, nor anything taken from it: and God doeth it, that men should fear before him (Ecc. 3:14).

Since on the infallible authority of the Holy Scripture and universally acknowledged Providence of God, "the earth is the LORD'S and the fulness thereof," has not God, the Divine and true Proprietor of the world with all its ponderous forces and mystic laws and every man in it by creation, the absolute right to give His possession and land to anyone He chooses? In the rhetoric of the parable of the vineyard, the LORD of the earth and creation would rightly argue his case at the bar of the world—a vindication of His final decision, saying: "Is it not lawful for me to do what I will with mine own?" (St. Matt. 20:15). Verily, verily, it is lawful for God the great Landowner to give any part of His possession to whomever He will! Because He chose to give it to Abraham and his seed forever, should Arabs, the descendants of Ishmael, or any other race

59

be envious and with discontent take up vociferous argument against the Creator, censure and criticize Allah Almighty for His decision, showing ill-will to their neighbors instead of rejoicing in their welfare? "Nay but, O man, who art thou that," chargest God, the Supreme Owner, with injustice and partiality? God has done nothing unjust—neither is there anything unlawful nor injurious in His sovereign act. If in the remote possibility there was partiality, it was in favor of Ishmael's descendants—the Arabs.

> And as for Ishmael, I have heard thee: Behold, I have blessed him, and will make him fruitful, and will multiply him exceedingly; twelve princes shall he beget, and I will make him a great nation.
> But my covenant will I establish with Isaac, which Sarah shall bear unto thee (Gen. 17:20-21).

The descendants of Ishmael have become a great people with a league of fourteen nations, numbering nearly 100,000,000, in the Middle East: while Israel is less than 3,000,000. So God has fulfilled His promise to the Arabs as well as to Israel.

The argument of the Arabs is that, they too are Abrahamic seed. The promise covers both in the seed of Father Abraham, but God specifies by saying: "my covenant will I establish with Isaac, which Sarah shall bear unto thee."

> And Sarah saw the son of Hagar the Egyptian, which she had born unto Abraham, mocking
> Wherefore she said unto Abraham, Cast out this bond-woman and her son: for the son of this bondwoman shall not be heir with my son, even with Isaac (Gen. 21:9-10).
> For it is written, that Abraham had two sons, the one by a bondmaid, the other by a freewoman.
> But he who was of the bondwoman was born after the flesh; but he of the freewoman was by promise.
> Nevertheless what saith the Scripture? Cast out the bond-

woman and her son: for the son of the bondwoman shall not be heir with the son of the freewoman (Gal. 4:22-23, 30).

The ultimate intent and logic of these Holy Scriptures in Aristotle's and Plato's distinguished categorical syllogism is that: *No child of a bondwoman can be an heir. Ishmael was the child of a bondwoman. Therefore, Ishmael cannot be an heir to Palestine.* This is the supreme posture of these inspired passages of Mosaic and Paulene origin.

When the Jewish State was destroyed by the Romans and the Jewish people were dispersed all over the world, Palestine was not left without Jews. A remnant remained in the Holy Land and clung persistently to the country. These were reinforced from time to time by immigrants from the Dispersion. Thus a Jewish community was in existence through all the centuries of the Great Dispersion, dwelling amidst the ruins and desolations of the land, but holding on passionately—a link in the chain of the past and the future—until the dispersed would return home.

During all this period of nearly 2000 years, Palestine was not even a name on the political map of the world. It was a portion of a larger province, Roman, Byzantine, Seljuk or Ottoman Turks, Crusaders, Mamelukes, Arabs, and its people were never conscious of themselves as a national unit. At no time in the whole recorded history of Palestine was the country one independent political state except under the Jews. When at the end of the 19th century the Jews began to return to the country with renewed dedication of the praying and patriot Nehemiah to rebuild the National Homeland, Palestine once more emerged from obscurity. "The Jews are the only people who ever made Palestine a national and political entity." But scarcely the present State of Israel had begun to crawl when the Arab hostility to drive the Jews into the Sea began. Under constant and violent pressure and peril, threatened with injury, Israel sang this poignant and ancient prayer passionately.

61

"Keep not thou silence, O God: hold not thy peace, and be not still, O God.

For, lo, thine enemies make a tumult: and they that hate thee have lifted up the head.

They have taken crafty counsel against thy people, and consulted against thy hidden ones.

They have said, Come, and let us cut them off from being a nation; that the name of Israel may be no more in remembrance.

For they have consulted together with one consent: they are confederate against thee:

The tabernacles of Edom, and the Ishmaelites; of Moab, and the Hagarenes;" (Ps. 83:1-6).

·There are students of political science, sociologists and demographers of varying sympathies specializing in the affairs of the Levant, who are intrigued with Palestine, now smothered with Arab-Israeli hostilities. They take part against and charge Israel with the offense coloring the account for the dramatic displacement of the Arab population. This most unfavorable and anti-Israel emotionalism, avarice and inhumanity of the sovereign Hebrew nation is a distortion of historical facts and far from categorical. The inescapable truth is that the Arab refugees were not driven out of Palestine as some would have us believe. Israel did not dismiss, expel or exile the Arabs from their habitation. They did not remove landmarks and claim as their own a neighbor's heritage; did not drive into their pastures flocks that were not theirs; did not take away the one ass of the fatherless and the one ox the widow had for ploughing her scanty fields, and with high hand did not overwhelm the Arab people of Palestine within their reach. The Arabs themselves at the instigation and master-minding of the hot-eyed Hadji-Emin-el-Husseini, the Grand Mufti and Shaikh-ul-Islam of Jerusalem; the notorious collaborator of Adolph Hitler, and supreme head of Palestine's 600,000 Moslems voluntarily made the exodus and left the land to flee the battle zone to facilitate by the military the destruction of Israel. They were called out of the Jewish areas with the glowing and extravagant promises in great presumption and the daring pledge that within three weeks they would return to their possession and indeed more, after the Jews in a vile sneer were driven to the swelling sea, as meat for the dragons of the deep. Instead, the Arabs themselves and their mechanized armies were dramatically driven and thrown back by the "feeble Jews" of dogmatic vigor with tragic consequences for many Arabs. They found themselves in a kind of exile, victims of knavery, creatures of chaotic influences tossed about on the waves of hopeless existence, making life a bewildering maze, a phantasmagoria of human struggle and defeat. Heaven seems to have called for it and earth to have obeyed the summons. Israel's ancient chant has it that the wicked are "like the chaff which the wind driveth away."

The unprecedented and appallingly vile scheme of driving the Jews into the sea, blind to the equity of their cause, in a wine cup of religious fury, originated with Mufti and his supreme council. Hitler himself in a blustering rage, like a savage lion that tears and devours, madly resolved to drive and drown the British army in the English Channel. While he aimed to exterminate the Jews with brimstone and fire in the German death-ovens, Hadji Emin, an arrogant modern "Samaritan Sanballat," plotted it with a massive burial of the Jews in the watery grave of the inky Mediterranean.

An impeccably clear proof, and the stamp and evidence of the truth on the contrary, is that instead of being driven, more than 300,000 Arabs, mainly Druzes, accepted the historical opportunity at the invitation and good-will of the Jews and stayed. They are today among the enterprising citizens sharing the fortunes and faith of Semitic genius of that sturdy and indestructible Messianic nation of Israel which, in this critical hour, with coals of fire in its heart is providing a home for God's suffering flock and homeless children in the Old Testament home of the seed of Abraham. (Psalm 105:6.)

In his unprecedented letter to a Black September fighter, Nathan Yalim-Mor in *Middle East International* says: "I was still a kid. But I had already my personal perturbations. All my Christian playmates sided with one or another of the belligerents. Among them I was the only outcast. My family was afraid of each of the fighting forces. I asked, Why is it so? The grown-up explained to me that we live not on our own land. We have one they said, but it is far away. Why shouldn't we return to this land? We shall go there one day, when the Messiah will take us there, by the will of God."

The chosen people of the covenant-keeping God are back in their promised land to prepare the way for the coming Messiah the Christ of God, the Son of Man, the Savior of the world: no mean rosewater eschatology.

This is not a vague piece of moralizing; but we believe, Allah be praised, that both Arabs and Israel with an over-whelming sense realize that war no longer is the answer. Therefore, Arab friends, in this time fraught with greatest significance, tear up the tents of deep resentment, hasty passion, heady and heated rhetoric of hatred against Israel and put your Semitic genius, capable of finest achievement, to work together. Lofty place where God makes peace. "At this turning point of history," the letter above continues, "there is only one choice: either to admit the other party's right to coexistence as a neighboring independent national body, or our two nations will go on escalating to unforeseeable dimen-sions. We are bound by a common fate—either to live together or to die together in futile wars." Gamal Abdul Nasser himself concluded before his death "that there could be no lasting military settlement." So, Arab friends, no longer consider Israel as conquerors; but rather accept them as neighbors who have returned to their God-ordained homeland, and recognize Israel's right to exist as a brother. Although the psychological barrier between Arab and Israeli has been built up over a quarter of a century of conflict, the futile upheaval and level of hostilities need not continue. *Having given the world a lesson in the arts of war, both Arabs and Jews ought to be now ready and eager to learn the arts of peace.* The sure promise to Abraham, who is the father of both Arab and Israeli is a promise to the seed of both. Therefore; the Arabs and Israelis, the children of Abraham can coexist as they have for generations: because they complement each other traditionally, religiously, culturally, speaking each other's language, and economically, trading and buying each other's goods. Thus they can be a blessing one to another in a healthy and happy relationship, forming a perfect community with dignity.

"Peaceful coexistence," said a discerning Arab in sober realism, "has its own dynamics." The choice then is yours, oh children of Abraham; Arabs and Jews. Stakes loom high. Come, therefore, come ye travelers in travail for territory, and beneath the beckoning arms of Arab's Allah, sign a truce before Israel's Jehovah.

According to the United Press International from Canterbury, England, the World Council of Churches, representing 241 Protestant and Orthodox denominations, urgently backed the demands that Israel return the Arab lands conquered by them in the June War of 1967. The Central Committee supporting the Arab states on the occupied territory question pressed the implementation of the United Nations Security Council resolution of November 22, 1967. That resolution called on Israel to withdraw from land it has held since the above conflict. The whole civilized world too was monolithic in its demand for an Israeli withdrawal to unsafe and unrecognized borders in return for the Arabs' willingness to call the old armistice agreement a "peace treaty."

The essayers of this resolution, the United Nations Security Council, may not have known the Scriptural legacy that Israel is in possession of her rightful inheritance. It is however, incredible to think that these ecclesiastical luminaries, members of the World Council of Churches, were blindly ignorant of the Abrahamic Covenant. The so-called Arab lands from which Israel is urged to vacate and withdraw was deeded by

God, who owns "the world and the fulness thereof" to Abraham and his specific seed Isaac, forever. The land belongs to Israel and to Israel alone. It is her promised land by divine election to which she has returned. This sovereign Deed, this holy covenant between Yahveh and His people Israel cannot be abrogated, neither will it ever wear out.

Albert Isterro, an Arab apologist, general secretary, Near East Council of Churches, Beirut, Lebanon, speaking on the subject immediately at hand, writes: "It is difficult for me to accept the idea that this 'event' "—meaning the restoration and return of the children of Israel to their Promised Land— "is a fulfillment of Biblical prophecy." Ah, but it is! All one needs to do to be convinced is to turn to the "Book unlike any other book," the Holy Bible, the only and supreme source of authoritative information about the people or the land. This extraordinary historical phenomenon, the physical rehabilitation of the land of Israel is the first and last act of God. According to God's divine distribution of nations it is their home—an inalienable possession from which they were dispersed by force. The book vividly records: "I will take you from among the nations, and gather you out of all the countries, and will bring you into *your own land*. Behold, I will take the children of Israel from among the nations, whither they are gone, and will gather them on every side, and bring them into *their own land*" (Ez. 36:24, 37:21). It is germane to note that the predetermined and monumental possessive case in these monosyllables, "their own land," is not a human invention but the decisive declaration of the El Shaddai— Almighty God Himself: "I will take you and will bring you into your own land." It is an integral part of God's continuing effort to achieve a physical extension of His firm promise, because it belongs not to men but to God Himself.

Our friend the Arab apologist, to justify his distilled dilemma offers a second argument by saying that the "Bible does not give definite geographical boundaries for such a promised land. On the contrary—the boundaries of this so-called 'Promised Land' are continually expanding in all directions."

The first part of this argument is so lucidly and explicitly defined in the Abrahamic Covenant above that "the wayfaring men, though fools shall not err therein," much less a general secretary of Council of Churches. This Covenant reads: "from the River of Egypt [Nile] unto the great River Euphrates, . . . from the desert, [Saudi-Arabian desert] even unto the Sea of the Philistines [Mediterranean]," leading to three continents: Asia, Africa and Europe. Concerning the continuing expansion of boundaries, there is little to argue with our Arab apologist. He is eminently right. It will continue to expand and extend, openly, not by stealth, until the historic boundaries under King David and Solomon from the Nile to Euphrates will become anew the kingdom of Israel; a just retribution and reward for generations of oppression, "And they shall dwell therein, . . . even they, and their children, and their children's children forever" (Ez. 37:25). The twelve tribes of Israel will reoccupy Palestine, which will be divided afresh among them, and enlarged from the Mediterranean and to the Nile, to the Euphrates and Persian Gulf (Ez. 47:13-21). Therefore no division of Palestine by the United Nations or any other international body will succeed, except the division made by God to the twelve tribes of Israel.

Then will the LORD drive out all these nations from before you, and ye shall possess greater nations and mightier than yourselves.

Every place wherein the soles of your feet shall tread shall be yours: from the wilderness and Lebanon, from the river, the river Euphrates, even unto the uttermost sea shall your coast be.

There shall no man be able to stand before you: for the LORD your God shall lay the fear of you upon all the land that ye shall tread upon, as he hath said unto you (Deut. 11:23-25).

Here then, is Israel's sovereignty and territorial integrity forever! Here then is the irrefutable and incontestable record of a divinely authoritative deed that Abraham was given in the eighteenth century before Christ, that the title of the land belongs to Israel. It is to be an everlasting possession of Abraham and his seed. And, significantly, it merits recording that this area, the historic boundaries, were the dominion of Hebrew monarchs, David and Solomon his son, both of whom reigned over it. It is true that the uninterrupted *possession* of the promised land by Israel depended upon her faithfulness to God's covenant with her. But Israel's *ownership* of the land, her title to it, was never to be affected by her conduct. The covenant was a contract between two parties: Abraham and God Himself. Moreover, Canaan has never been without the presence of Jews, and Israel was already settled in Canaan when the land was conquered by Joshua in 1230 B.C. The Abrahamic Covenant was, therefore, irrevocable. This, then, is not a Jewish drive for *Lebensraum* or Zionist policy of annexation or expansion by conquest of Arab lands, but coming into possession of their God-owned and God-ordained homeland. The land was God's before Arabs ever existed and He gave it to a people whom He chose as His own. Unto this people of Israel God spoke in poignant tone:

> O thou afflicted, tossed with tempest. . . .
> for a small moment I have forsaken thee: but with great mercies will I gather thee (Isa. 54:7, 11) (Ez. 34:11-13, 36:24, 37:21).
>
> No weapon that is formed against thee shall prosper; and every tongue that shall rise against thee in judgment shalt thou condemn. This is the heritage of the servants of the LORD, and their righteousness is of me, saith the LORD (Isa. 54:17).

Nothing could be clearer than the holy promise made in these passages that perpetual possession of the land of Canaan was God's guarantee to Israel regardless of their conduct and behaviour. Palestine was promised divinely to Israel in perpetuity!

> I will surely assemble, O Jacob, all of thee; I will surely gather the remnant of Israel; I will put them together as the sheep of Bozrah, and the flock in the midst of their fold; (Micah 2:12).

It is indeed a wonder to behold the children of Israel again flocking to their fatherland, and their nationality recognized by the powers whose governments in the past grievously oppressed them. Commenting on this prophecy by prophet Micah, "In our sight and in our days," said David Ben Gurion, then prime minister of Israel,

> the scattered people is homing from every corner of the globe and every point of the compass, out of all nations among which it was cast away, and it is coursing over its Land, over Israel redeemed. We live and die for a Messianic ideal, the advanced guard of universal redemption. Through generations untold, we, and no other people believed in the vision of the last days. It cannot be that a vision which for so long inspired a people's faith, its hope and patient expectancy will disappoint it now of all times, when the miracle which is the State of Israel has come to pass. Today as we renew our independence, our first concern must be to build up the Land. But these are the whereby not the end. The end is a State fulfilling prophecy, bringing Salvation to all men.

What has secured the survival of the Jewish people through the grim generations, and led to the creation of the state is the Messianic vision of the prophets of Israel, the vision of redemption for the Jewish people and for all humanity. The ingathering and restoration of the remnant of Israel to its promised land is the beginning of the realization of the Messianic vision.

With the approval of the Chief Rabbinate of the state of

69

Israel, the following prayer is recited on the anniversary of the independence of the state of Israel. "May it be Thy will, O Jehovah our God and the God of our fathers, that as we have been granted the dawn of redemption, so we may be granted to hear the trumpet of the Messiah. We shall sing before Him a New Song. Hallelujah."

O ye seed of Abraham his servant, ye children of Jacob his chosen,

He is the LORD our God: his judgments are in all the earth.

He hath remembered his covenant forever.

Which covenant he made with Abraham, and his oath unto Isaac;

And confirmed the same unto Jacob for a law, and to Israel for an everlasting covenant:

Saying, Unto thee will I give the land of Canaan, the lot of your inheritance:

When they were but a few men in number; yea, very few, and strangers in it.

When they went from one nation to another, from one kingdom to another people;

For he remembered his holy promise, and Abraham his servant.

And he brought forth his people with joy, and his chosen with gladness;

And gave them the lands of the heathen: and they inherited the labour of the people;

That they might observe his statutes, and and keep his laws. Praise ye the LORD (PS. 105:6-13, 42-45).

After lapse, hopes and fears, "sweat, blood and tears" of two thousand years, in accordance with the Balfour Declaration in 1917; "His Majesty's government—views with favor the establishment in Palestine of a national home for the Jewish people"; the 1923 League of Nations's mandate to

Britain, and the 1947 decision of the United Nations, Israel declared national independence. The state of Israel became a reality, when on May 14, 1948, in the little white marble Art Museum, thirty-seven members of the Jewish Provincial Council headed by Chairman David Ben Gurion, valiant warrior and scholar, who in 929 words messianically proclaimed, at the classic hour of 4:00 P.M., that "Next year Jerusalem's dream" was fulfilled. Golda Meir, Israel's indestructible and archetypal Jewish heroine, the present prime minister and flinty leader was one of them.

With this extraordinary historical phenomenon begins the day of grim challenge for nationhood and struggle to heal the centuries of dispersion under the Star of David. Premier Ben Gurion, in fulfillment of Old Testament prophecy of the ingathering of exiles; "Operation Magic Carpet Airlift," sent his messengers to Yemen, saying; "We are sending aeroplanes for you." The Yemenite Jews did not know what an aeroplane was. When they saw the planes of El Al Israel Airlines they refused to get on board until the rabbis read Exodus 19:4; "I bare you on eagles' wings and brought you to myself," and from the prophecy of Isaiah (63:9) that God would send for them and carry them home on the wings of eagles. The Rabbis assured them: "Little Ones, God is sending His eagles for His children." Then these little Yemenite Jews climbed on without hesitation and fear. More than 50,000 Jews came home to Israel without the loss of a single child in this great airlift; not even the infants that were born in flight.

An old Rabbi of eighty-five years of age was asked, what was his dream, what did he want most in the world? He answered; "I want three things: first, I want to see Israel developed; second, I want to live long enough to see peace; third, I want to see the Messiah with my own eyes."

The Jews have been pouring into the Holy Land, 1,275,000 of them from seventy-five nations and every level of culture and civilization, since the country became independent:

swarthy, burnoose-clad Orientals from Iraq, Iran, Kurdistan and Morocco; scores of thousands of homeless from Germany and Eastern Europe; people from countries as diverse as India, Syria and the Soviet Union. After two thousand years of wandering, this is sometimes looked upon as an abnormal mass psychology, a politically romantic movement; but after the fulfillment of these Messianic prophecies and lucid light of eschatological expectancy who can doubt that this spiritual national tendency and series of events in history are the acts of God embodying a purpose of eternal quality to reunite Israel with Himself in the cradle of the nation. With their deathless yearning for the land of their fathers, and belief of future rest and greatness there after all their wanderings, how visibly do they seem to feel that a change for them and their condition has at last come.

> As pleasing odor I will accept you, when I bring you out from the peoples, and gather you out of the countries where you have been scattered; and I will manifest My holiness among you in the sight of the nations. And you shall know that I am the LORD when I bring you into the land of Israel, the country which I swore to give to your fathers (Ez. 20:41-42).

From this intensifying sign we see that God is not yet done with the Jews. There are those who tell us that all God's promises to Israel are dead, never again to be revived. But the giver and maker of these promises and covenants does not so speak. The inspired Apostle, even after Jerusalem had fallen, wrote in reference to this very subject, that "the gifts and calling of God are without repentance"; and that for Israel which has been cast down and broken, there is a coming fulness, recovery and restoration for this marvelous race today. How else can their unparalleled history of preservation be explained—with such unwaning and ever-active life-energy, against overwhelming odds and storms of centuries and bloody persecutions of so many generations, amid the wrecks of many buried empires? How else can that undying presentiment be understood, which throbs in the universal Jewish heart, and which no adversity can quench or prosperity entirely charm into quiet of some future return to the high estate of their fathers? The very land itself, in its perpetual refusal to give peaceful and secure home to any of the Gentiles who have overrun it, throughout all its sad desolations, gives out its plaints and prayers that Jehovah would not forget His covenant with the house of Israel, and utters from every hill and valley, shore and sea, the prophecy of some future hope and blessing which cannot be delayed forever.

General Allenby was the Christian hero of the first World War whom God used so miraculously for the conquest of Jerusalem without the firing of a single gun. Students of history and our readers will remember the brilliant reception and ovation given the field marshal at the Royal Albert Hall in London at the close of World War I, in appreciation for his phenomenal achievements in the Holy Land campaigns. On that occasion, the general made an epochal address. He told how as a little boy brought up in the highlands of Scotland he had knelt at his mother's knee night after night to say his evening prayers; and as he was taught from his earliest memories to lisp after his mother the closing part of the prayer, "And, O Lord, we would not forget thine ancient people, Israel; hasten the day when Israel shall again be thy people and shall be restored to thy favor and to their land." Then, holding back the tears with great difficulty, he said humbly and simply, "I never knew that God would give me the privilege to answer my own childhood prayers!"

Rabbi Kalisher, a highly educated rabbi of Polish origin, steeped in rabbinic lore and secular subjects as well; sought to prove from the Bible, that not only is it God's will that Jews should reestablish themselves in their ancient homeland but that the Messiah would not come until the Jews had first prepared the way for Him by rebuilding the land to which He is to come. This is the ultimate meaning and message of the Jewish Sign. The Messiah of Rabbi Kalisher, whose First Coming he eagerly awaits, is the believer's "blessed Hope and the glorious appearing of the great God and our Saviour, Jesus Christ" (Titus 2:13).

Nations are shaking, while hungered hearts yearn
Israel's awaking; awaiting MESSIAH's return;
Sorely threatened the city, the state;
Against hostile forces they still guard the gate.

Stranger, thy people have wandered afar,
Though hated and hunted, they ne'er lost hope
    in their Star;
Blasted and broken, but building again
Bound by the Promise of blessing to men.

For GOD is faithful; His Covenant still
Waits on His people His plan to fulfill;
Desert doth blossom; the dry bones do live:
Oppressed ones of Jehovah their allegiance still give!

PRAY FOR THE PEACE OF JERUSALEM! PRAY!
JESUS—MESSIAH—IS COMING SOME DAY!
SLOW OF HEART AWAKE!
    PROMISED POWER RELEASE!
PRAY FOR JERUSALEM! DAVID'S CITY OF PEACE!

V

WHY THE LORD DELAYETH HIS COMING

Just before the final and holy benediction with which ends the apocalypse, indeed the Holy Bible itself, the enthroned Christ "on the right hand of the Majesty on high" proclaimed:

> Behold, I come quickly; and my reward is with me, to give every man according as his work shall be (Rev. 22:12).

Intangible wonder that believers, at best humans, with poignancy ask; why delayeth He His coming, seeing that all signs of the times do so eloquently point to its imminent fulfillment?

Saint Peter, the chief spokesman to whom the Lord, in response to his great confession, "Thou art Christ, the Son of the living God," gave "the keys of the kingdom of heaven," exhorts believers to godly patience and inspires them with the certainty of Christ's coming in judgment.

> The Lord is not slack concerning his promise, as some men count slackness; but is longsuffering to us-ward, not willing that any should perish, but that all should come to repentance (II Peter 3:9).

These holy oracles, embodying the revelation concerning the day of the Lord, need no interpretation. It is for us the students of the Word to know and understand that the sovereign Lord has neither forgotten his unfailing promises, nor is there any power in heaven nor on earth which can prevent Him from fulfilling His Covenant to the Church. All the prophecies and divine promises concerning His first advent were gloriously fulfilled; so also the promises as to His

Second Coming will be fulfilled, word for word.

There have been occasions in the history of nations, such as happened once in the British Empire. The king was scheduled for a visit to Australia, a member of the United Kingdom. A most elaborate preparation, befitting a welcome to a royal personage, having been completed and perfected with national flags, streamers and buntings to give the city a gala appearance, the citizens and subjects from far and near had waited breathlessly while the bands played national airs for the king's arrival. All this was done to enhance the glory of the king. That day was in a very special sense his day, because he was the king, and therefore a day of natural rejoicing also. At the last minute an unprecedented hindrance made it impossible for the sovereign to keep his appointment. The vast multitude that had thronged the festively adorned avenue to share in its glory and happiness, being deeply disappointed, returned to their accustomed way of life. The Lord Jesus, Lord of heaven and earth, is not a mortal man to be held back by mundane circumstances nor impeded by human limitations in His conquering march. Not so with Him! Not even the gates of hell shall prevail against His divine plans, against the royal glory of His coming. But as we have noticed in the above Petrine passage, it is only man's persistence in sin and peoples' unrepentant way of life and scoffers who scorn, "Where is the promise of his coming?" "Where is the God of judgment?" (Mal. 2:17), that keep Him from returning. No power on earth can delay His coming in victory as the hope of perishing and long-suffering humanity.

The "delay indicates, not that he is behind the clock, but the quality of his purpose—namely, the fact that the moment of closure is entirely subordinate to the yearning and patience of a love" for souls. Lo, my soul, here is the reason why the Lord delayeth His coming; not because He is not ready, not because He encountered opposition or hindrance, but because men and women are still in their sin. They have not passed from death unto life, they have not been translated out of darkness into the marvelous light of God's dear Son. You see, oh do you see, that He is not willing that any should perish. And we need not perish because He purchased our soul's salvation at a great price—His death and resurrection a salvation of universal attainment bejewelled in the promise: "Him that cometh to me I will in no wise cast out" (St. John 6:37). The Lord delayeth His coming, because He waits for men to repent of their sin and return to Him, the rightful King of souls.

Apostle Peter assigns another reason why the Lord delayeth His coming. This time he directs his message to believers. "Seeing then that . . . ye are looking for the coming of the day of God, what manner of persons ought ye to be in all holy conversation and godliness" (II Peter 3:11-12). The believers who pray: "Even so come, Lord Jesus," should understand that His soon coming is governed by their watchful readiness. They can hasten His coming through righteousness and holy preparedness, as a bride adorns herself for the bridegroom. This means an inner separation for the believer from the world.

> Love not the world, neither the things that are in the world. If any man love the world, the love of the Father is not in him.
> For all that is in the world, the lust of the flesh, and the lust of the eyes, and the pride of life, is not of the Father, but is of the world.
> And the world passeth away, and the lust thereof: but he that doeth the will of God abideth forever (I John 2:15-17).

In speaking to the believers who look for union with Christ, now and hereafter, Saint Paul the chief apostle adds his own admonition:

> If ye then be risen with Christ, seek those things which are above, where Christ sitteth on the right hand of God.

Set your affection on things above, not on things on earth. For ye are dead, and your life is hid with Christ in God. When Christ, who is our life, shall appear, then shall ye also appear with him in glory (Col. 3:1-4).

Until, esteemed reader, these two cardinal conditions are met, the Lord will delay His coming. In the meantime He is making no needless delay. To the question of the Church, "O Lord, how long?" He answers: "Quickly." Therefore, we must be continually braced up by the thought that it may be EVEN NOW!

> See Redemption, long expected,
>   In transcendent pomp appear—
> All his saints by men rejected,
>   Throng in gathering legions near:
> Melt, ye mountains! melt, ye mountains!
>   Into smoke, for God is here.

According to the prophetic calendar, the true attitude of the Church, is to be looking and ready any day and every day for the Coming of Christ to seize away His waiting and watching saints. But in faithfully assuming this attitude, and thus hoping and expecting the speedy fulfillment of what has been promised, the Church has been made to see one notable period after another pass away without bringing the realization of the consummation which was anticipated. When saintly Simeon took the infant Saviour to his bosom and sang his exulting Nunc Dimittis, he supposed that the time for the consummation had arrived, but it was only the preliminary advent that he had lived to see. When the intrepid and dauntless John the Baptist, a preacher with divine afflatus thundered his vigorous calls to repentance and inner renewal through the rocky defiles of Judea, the joyous burden of his soul and message was, that now the consummator was come with winnowing fan to make the final separation between the chaff and the wheat; but what was foremost in his contemplation was yet a score of centuries off. Early Christians were lively in their expectations that in their day the standard of the coming Lord would be seen unfurled in the sky, and all their hopes be fulfilled; but the days of the Apostles and the apostolic fathers passed, and still "the Bridegroom tarried." Nearly every century, as it rolled by, was designated as the one in which the Church might confidently count on being translated from earth to heaven; but each, like the one before it, came to an end, without ushering in that most notable event on which our eyes are ever to be fixed. The great Reformation itself, with the revival of the primitive faith, revived the primitive hope, that the great day must needs be very close at hand; but the days of the celebrated Reformers and scholars passed, and all the days which they designated; and yet the momentous day had not arrived.

Though the apocalypse of Jesus Christ and His coming with power and great glory might seem slow, delay after delay, it is necessary for the preservation of the faith of God's people to hear the fresh edict from the lips of their Lord, that "there shall be no more delay." He will come. There is not another truth in God's Word that is so peculiarly and powerfully authenticated. All the holy prophets since the world began have foretold it. All the Apostles and evangelists have inwrought it in all their writings as one of the central and fixed doctrines in the divine plan of salvation. Our Lord Jesus Himself has given us parable on parable, and promise upon promise, all comprehensive of this one truth. And God hath certified it to all men, in that He hath raised up Christ from the dead. But after all the rest of the canon of inspiration was finished, another book was indited, making this its particular and specific theme; in which the mighty Judge himself appears, and gives forth the most intense and awful affirmation on the solemn subject. With clouds for his garments and the rainbow for his crown—with his countenance shining as the sun and his feet glowing like pillars of fire—with a roll in his hand, lifted by his merit from the throne of infinite majesty, he stretches up his right hand into the sky, and swears—swears by the Eternal—swears by the power which has given birth and being to all things—that, in spite of all the mistakes, disappointments, delays, and consequent doubts upon the subject, that the time shall come when there shall be no more delay!

True as the life of God—certain as the Divine eternity—unfailing as the power which made the worlds—immutable as the oath of Jesus—the great crowning day will come, when the whole mystery of God shall be fulfilled. Away then with unbelief! Misgiving, be thou buried in the depths of the sea! Doubt, be thou dissolved into everlasting shame! "Behold, He cometh with clouds, and every eye shall see Him, and they which pierced Him. Even so, Amen."

VI

WHY THE LORD WILL COME AGAIN

The Anglo-Saxon race has been called the most questioning and doubting member of the human family. But no matter what one's beginning and ethnic origin might happen to be, man is a questioning creature. He questions everything; theology and religion are no exceptions. So there are those unprepared minds and unstretched imaginations in our contemporary social system who shyly ask: "Why will the Lord Jesus Christ come again?" The authority for our answer is recorded in two passages of God's Word. To the troubled and saddened disciples, because of His going away and separation, Jesus spoke the comforting words:

> Let not your heart be troubled: ye believe in God, believe also in me.
> In my Father's house are many mansions; if it were not so, I would have told you. I go to prepare a place for you.
> And if I go and prepare a place for you, I will come again, and receive you unto myself; that where I am there ye may be also (St. John 14:1-3).

The angel of the Lord in announcing His first advent said, "Thou shalt call his name JESUS; for he shall save his people from their sins" (St. Matt. 1:21). This was the message of the angel, and this was the supreme mission of Jesus: to save people from their sins. He accomplished this great salvation by shedding his precious blood on the Cross of Calvary, aware of the solemn fact that "without shedding of blood there is no remission of sins." So the apostle in exhorting believers to a life of holiness can write:

> Forasmuch as ye know that ye were not redeemed with corruptible things, as silver and gold, from your vain conversation received by tradition from your fathers;
>
> But with the precious blood of Christ, as of a lamb without blemish and without spot:
>
> Who verily was foreordained before the foundation of the world, but was manifest in these last times for you (I Peter 1:18-20).

He by the grace of God tasted death for every man. God the Father accepted the sacrifice and raised Him from the dead. Now He is exalted in heaven and sitteth at the right hand of God the Father Almighty from whence He shall come to judge the quick and the dead; He will bring the Church of God which He had purchased with His own blood that they may share His glory in heaven.

Once upon a time a man in the mute eloquence and stillness of cold winter was toiling in his garden plot. A friend passing by remarked, "You've engaged yourself to a tough job in that frozen ground, haven't you?"

"But ah," answered the gardener, "the Spring is at hand, and that prospect fills me with thrills of joy." So is it with the godly, the true believer in future blessedness. For every child of God, the prospect of an endless life of glory in heaven with all the company of the redeemed saints does away with present hardship and difficulties. This is what the veteran apostle had in mind, when he exhorted young Timothy to constancy and perseverance, saying: "If we suffer we shall also reign with him."

> Seeing it is a righteous thing with God to recompense tribulation to them that trouble you;
>
> And to you who are troubled rest with us, when the Lord Jesus shall be revealed from heaven with his mighty angels.
>
> In flaming fire taking vengeance on them that know not God, and that obey not the gospel of our Lord Jesus Christ:
>
> Who shall be punished with everlasting destruction from

the presence of the Lord, and from the glory of his power;
When he shall come to be glorified in his saints, and to be admired in all them that believe (II Thess. 1:6-10).

The above passages make abundantly clear and leave no room for doubt as to the reason and purpose why the Lord will come again. Since, "from the days of John the Baptist until now the kingdom of heaven suffereth violence"; injustice, persecutions and tribulations have been leveled by the world against the innocent and the godly. In the world ye shall have tribulation, said Jesus, and you shall be honored with martyrdoms, like the Armenians, the people of the first Christian kingdom; who became the victims of the first genocide of the twentieth century, on their native soil in western Armenia, with the martyrdom of two million people whose authentic witness for Christian faith and martyrdom have put the Church and the civilized world under the heaviest debt and obligation for all that Christianity and culture comprehends! For a time of cosmic conflict, how comforting and encouraging are the promises of the enthroned Saviour to the Church on trial on earth; but be of good cheer; I have overcome the world. "Be thou faithful unto death, and I will give thee a crown of life" (Rev. 2:10). For a little while men may continue to rebel against God's laws and order, as though the Almighty does not exist—"dead." All this is so because the Lord is patient and long-suffering. But He neither forgets nor sleepeth. He patiently bides His time.

But the day cometh, that shall burn as an oven; and all the proud, yea, and all that do wickedly, shall be stubble: and the day that cometh shall burn them up, saith the Lord of hosts that shall leave them neither root nor branch (Mal. 4:1).
But who may abide the day of his coming? and who shall stand when he appeareth? for he is like a refiner's fire, and like fuller's soap:
And he shall sit as a refiner and purifier of silver: and he

shall purify the sons of Levi, and purge them as gold and silver, that they may offer unto the Lord an offering in righteousness (Mal. 3:2-3).

He will establish His Kingdom forever and will reign in righteousness, holiness and peace, when He shall come to be glorified in His saints, and be admired in all them that believe. They who watched, they who waited, they who prayed, "Even so come, Lord Jesus," will share His glory and majesty forever. This is why the Lord Jesus will come again!

The first promise of the Second Coming of Christ, comprehensive of His incarnation and victory over Satan, was made at the beginning of Creation in the Garden of Eden to the woman that her seed should bruise the serpent's head. This exceeding great and precious promise in the first book of the Holy Bible opens the door of "that blessed hope, and the glorious appearing of the great God and our Saviour Jesus Christ." This highway of redemption for the human race, "dead in trespasses and sins" by bruising Satan's head must be fulfilled. The fulfilment of that promise and prophecy is recorded in Revelation (20:2): the last book of the Bible; when our Lord in the plentitude of His mighty power, by the hand of an angel from heaven binds Satan for a thousand years under His feet and the feet of His saints.

As the final bruising of the serpent's head will take place at the Second Coming, and the promise of the bruising is made in Eden, then the first promise of the coming is made in Eden. So we hear for the first time the story and the doctrine of the Second Coming of the Second Man; and thus the story and the doctrine of the Second Coming begin with the very beginning of the Book. This is why He is coming.

Yes! He will come.

He will descend from heaven with a shout of command. He will pass it on to Michael the archangel. The archangel will pass it on to the angel who is called the "trump of God." He will cause a sound, a blast, an utterance of power at which the doors of graves of every sort shall open outward, every secret hiding place of the purchased dead will be revealed, and the sacred dust will bloom with life. In the body of every regenerated soul there is planted the germ of the new body. Just as the buried grain of wheat is linked by the unseen air to the fructifying sun in heaven and at a given moment is quickened and comes forth in new form, so the nucleus of the new body is held by the Holy Spirit (of which the air is the symbol) to the risen, glorified body of the Son of God in heaven.

No matter what may befall the body in which it was buried it will abide to that hour we call the resurrection and transfiguration, and at the shout, the voice and action of the trump of God will come forth in the glow of unfolded and eternal beauty as the sheath, the house, the home, the perfect dwelling place, the royal robe of the souls the Lord shall bring with him; while the living shall flash forth in the same immortality and glory.

Yes! The dust of death shall bloom and mortality shall put on immortality at the coming of the Lord.

VII

MARANATHA—WHEN THE LORD COMETH

As we continue the study of the doctrine of the Lord's Second Coming, it is of the utmost importance for us to know what is our position and state, and especially, how should He find us. This is absolutely fundamental and therefore merits further consideration.

First of all, it is necessary to emphasize in no uncertain terms that our Lord, though He admonished His followers, "Occupy till I come," He never encouraged nor taught the believers to abandon their daily vocations and avocations, and merely wait for Him. Despite the very plain teaching and forewarning of the Lord that "that day and hour knoweth no man, no, not the angels in heaven, but my father only," many accents went unheeded and apocalyptists, under the leadership of fallible teachers of morbid curiosity and contradictory counsellors set dates, claiming that he will come on a certain day. The advocates of this determinism based their theory and argument on certain Biblical figures in the books of Daniel and of Revelation. Caught up in the current of this mechanical confusion many innocent families groping toward they knew not whither, sold their homes and properties to prepare themselves for the exciting event, only to find themselves and their assumption and conception of the way in which God directs history and exact time of Christ's return, hopelessly mistaken. Most naturally the devotees of this supposititious and speculative hypothesis found themselves in theological shoals upon which the faith of countless men and women have been shipwrecked. Confounded time and time again and scandalously humiliated, they stand at the bar of mockers and scoffers of the world in dumb resignation and despair. The fallacy of such mistaken magnitudes is that it often reduces the titanic into the trivial. In a time fraught with destiny when great thoughts of Christ's coming belt the globe, seeking open hearts to enter and alert minds, there are those as above, who ride as valiant knights on wooden horses. Such illusions require to be buried as deeply as a lost planet. "Who hath known the mind of the Lord? or who hath been his counsellor?" (Rom. 11:34). The ways of divine providence transcend the finite contemplation of human reason, and so man must rest in the wisdom of God.

The Lord in His infinite wisdom has kept that day secret and unknown to mortals. This knowledge is limited to the Father because He alone can determine the moment. In a special way He commended His disciples and believers in all ages of the Church, "Watch therefore: for ye know not what hour your Lord doth come" (St. Matt. 24:42). And this watching is to go hand in hand with honorable industry and fervency of spirit.

> Who then is a faithful and wise servant, whom his lord hath made ruler over his household, to give them meat in due season?
> Blessed is that servant, whom his lord when he cometh shall find so doing (St. Matt. 24:45-46).

Watchful Christians who expect the imminent coming of the Lord at any hour of the day will occupy themselves with fruitbearing acts and activity to the last moment.

Near a beautiful lake in Switzerland, away from sightseers' curious gaze, there was a garden. But one day a tourist turning around knocked on the gate of the garden. An elderly man opened the gate and cordially welcomed the stranger. The visitor noticed that the aged host was himself the gardener, while the master had returned home only four times in twenty-four years, the last being twelve years before. He asked the aged gardener, "Do you always manicure and meticulously maintain and care for this garden as if your master will come tomorrow?" The faithful gardener answered, "No, I aim to keep this garden in perfect condition as if my master will come today!" So it is with us. Our coming Lord and Master would have us be found in that same attitude of mind and spirit expectation for his sudden and sure coming today. Therefore, again and again He admonished, "watch and pray."

> Watch ye therefore: for ye know not when the master of the house cometh, at even or at midnight, or at the cock-crowing, or in the morning:
> Lest coming suddenly he find you sleeping.
> And what I say unto you I say unto all, Watch (St. Mark 13:35-37).

In this monosyllable and awesome little word "All" we are *all* included.

For some years there hung above my desk in gilded frame a beautiful painting of the ten virgins, presented to me in recognition of my humble and cooperative services in the erection of a Church building in suburban Boston. This haunting parable of our Lord's return, with which all students of the Holy Scriptures are familiar, is recorded in His Olivet discourse in the twenty-fifth chapter of the Gospel according to St. Matthew. Any Bible student who attempts a description of this poignant narrative, must "take off his shoes" because he stands on holy ground. Even then he must give it up as a hopeless task; for what man is he who can measure up to the Master who spoke as never man spoke, and in speaking adorned the Church with this matchless parable.

The artist with great and transcendent skill to give meaning and emotion, portrays the wise and foolish virgins, five on the right and five on the left making the all-comprehending figure number of ten. All ten have their lamps, but the lamps of the foolish virgins lacked oil: "They took no oil." It appears that they thought more of the going forth than of the meeting of the bridegroom. They altogether misapprehended the nature and the purpose of the mission they so cheerfully assumed. Their unpreparedness, therefore, ended in disappointment and appalling reversal of their hopes and realization of their worst fear. They missed the chance of meeting the bridegroom; they could not share in the marriage feast. To their tragic plea, wrapped up in a melancholy strain and mournful cry with clear sense of helplessness and loss, "Lord, Lord, open to us," the answer came from within, solemn and subdued, "I know you not." In these controlled and deeply impressive words one seems to hear the decisive and desolating doom of the lost.

Those who in the confidence of superior capacities or attainments, neglect the spiritual way of truth and life, should be reminded that nothing will supply the want of wisdom and prudence, but that negligence long continued will make knowledge useless and genius a folly.

The skilled craftsman of fine arts represents the five virgins who shaped their conduct by dressing in their best and laciest apparel and beautiful wedding garments each armed and adorned with flowers. Fully equipped, they go forth, holding aloft their "trimmed and burning lamps" firmly grasped, while the last one at the rear carries a vessel with extra supply of oil leaving no cause for fear of losing their lights. Ah, this means, esteemed reader, that vessel of oil is not enough without the burning lamp; nor the lamp merely lighted with no supply of oil. These that were thus watchful and ready by the time the bridegroom appeared met him and went in with him mingling at the marriage feast of exultant joy and gladness. Not only their lamps were bright with light, but their hearts were also lighted: inward readiness to meet the bridegroom of their soul.

This parable illustrates the state of the Christian Church on earth at the time of Christ's Second Advent. The ten virgins— five wise, and five foolish—who had previously taken their lamps and gone forth to meet the Bridegroom, but had fallen asleep while he tarried: "While the Bridegroom tarried they all slumbered and slept. And at midnight there was a cry made, Behold the Bridegroom cometh: go ye out to meet him." No words can be made more provocative or expressive than those to show that shortly before the personal return of Christ, all professing Christians are in general to be completely indifferent and silent about the positive and definite nearness of his return, without any deep-rooted conviction that his return is absolute and immediate, so slumbering and sleeping overtakes them in a state of spiritual darkness, described by Christ as that of *Midnight*. The Church indeed may be active and extremely zealous and successful in proclaiming other doctrines and parts of the Gospel, but in regard to the positive expectation of the imminent and personal coming of Christ, to which particular point the parable solely and exclusively refers, they are in a condition of midnight slumber.

This is remarkably the case in the torn modern Church life in rival camps, wrongly polarized between partial opinions. There are extremely few influential voices whose clear loud-sounding proclamation—definite prophetic messages with firm evangelical conviction in relation to the nearing Advent of Christ—to excite spiritual interest and general attention to the impending final crisis, are raised today. There are, indeed hosts of believers in the personal and premillennial Advent of Christ that may take place at any time, even within the lifetime of the present generation. But in the very midst of the present midnight darkness, coldness, indifference and silence, the Christian Church has allowed concern for Christ's Advent to pale into social action. To these unwatchful and lukewarm Christians of the Laodicean Church, there will suddenly arise on every side a piercing irresistible trumpet-tongued cry of warning that shall shake all Christians, foolish as well as wise to the infallible truths and astounding event of Christ's return "with power and great glory." The foolish virgins were not ready to go out into the midnight darkness and meet their returning Lord; they did not have the supply of divine truth to make their lamps burn when needed, and they are seeking it when they ought to have possessed it, and so are shut from the joys of the bridegroom's presence. Nevertheless, the Redeemer will approach this earth full of grace and compassion, and having quickly received to himself his waiting people and watchful Christians, will at joyous season entertain no other thoughts than of pity and compassion toward the foolish and benighted ones that are left behind.

> Rejoice, rejoice, believers,
>   And let your lights appear;
> The evening is advancing,
>   And darker night is near:
> The Bridegroom is arising,
>   And soon He draweth nigh;
> Up, pray, and watch, and wrestle,
>   At midnight comes the cry.
>
> See that your lamps are burning;
>   Replenish them with oil;
> And wait for your salvation,
>   The end of earthly toil.
> The watchers on the mountain
>   Proclaim the Bridegroom near,
> Go meet Him as He cometh,
>   With alleluias clear.
>
> Our Hope and Expectation,
>   O Jesus, now appear!
> Arise, Thou Sun so longed for,
>   O'er this benighted sphere!
> With hearts and hands uplifted,
>   We plead, O Lord, to see
> The day of earth's redemption
>   That brings us unto Thee.

The time of Christ's Second Coming as in the parable above, is unknown to us finites, but from the foregoing pages and infallible Biblical references and proofs, His great Advent is certain and strikingly, unmistakably sure. Ours as true children of God is to watch, not on our backs as stargazers, but like the wise virgins, in lively zeal have our lamps trimmed and oiled, and adorned with our wedding garments, heads up, hearts ready to answer the "midnight cry ... behold the bridegroom cometh; go ye out to meet him," "For yet a little while, and he that shall come will come, and will not tarry" (Hebrews 10:37).

> Not as of old, a little child,
> To bear, and fight and die,
> But crowned with glory like the sun
> That lights the morning sky.
>
> O brighter than that glorious morn
> Shall this fair morning be,
> When Christ our King in beauty comes
> And we His face shall see.

PAROUSIA, or THE RAPTURE OF THE SAINTS

The first stage in Christ's SECOND ADVENT into
"THE AIR" or Atmospheric heavens, the resurrection of
Saints and their ascension together with living and
watchful Christians to meet Christ in the heavens is
called in the New Testament, PAROUSIA (I Thess.
4:16-17, I Cor. 15:51).

VIII

PAROUSIA—THE RAPTURE OF THE SAINTS

What is Parousia or the Rapture? It is a matter of great importance to distinguish between the Parousia or actual presence of Christ in the atmospheric heavens at the first stage of His Advent and the epiphaneia or visible manifestation of that presence to the world. The word, parousia, is recorded twenty-four times, and the expression, epiphaneia, six times in the New Testament. This gem of a word, parousia, from the golden tongue of John Chrysostom is used sixteen times to express the coming of Christ. The first stage in Christ's Second Advent or the first half in a single process into "THE AIR" or atmospheric heavens and the resurrection of the bodies of all deceased saints and their ascension together with watchful living Christians to meet Christ in the heavens is called Parousia or the Rapture of the saints; the upward call of God in Christ Jesus. At the Rapture, as the word itself signifies, He will not descend to the earth; He only appears in the air. This is the appearance which the Holy Scripture describes as "a thief in the night."

> But of the times and the seasons, brethren, ye have no need that I write unto you.
> For yourselves know perfectly that the day of the Lord so cometh as a thief in the night (I Thess. 5:1-2).

The dramatically and breathtaking quick action of Rapture, "as the lightning cometh out of the east, and shineth unto the west, so shall also the coming of the Son of man be" (St. Matt. 24:27). This is described by Jesus and Apostle Paul, "Suddenly": "In a moment, in the twinkling of an eye" (I Cor.

15:52). In the Parousia, then, Christ shall come to catch away His bride secretly. Just as the sleeping world does not see the Morning Star, so the blind and rebellious people will be wholly unaware of the appearing of the bright and morning star, the Lord Jesus Christ. Only those who are looking for Him will see Him. Parousia or Rapture is therefore defined as the visible return from heaven of Jesus the Messiah for His Saints. The pattern of His arrival is awesomely pictured for our understanding in the eschatological passage below.

> For this we say unto you by the word of the Lord, that we which are alive and remain unto the coming of the Lord shall not prevent them which are asleep.
> For the Lord himself shall descend from heaven with a shout, with the voice of the archangel, and with the trump of God: and the dead in Christ shall rise first:
> Then we which are alive and remain shall be caught up together with them in the clouds, to meet the Lord in the air: and so shall we ever be with the Lord.
> Wherefore comfort one another with these words (I Thess. 4:15-18).

The Parousia will be like the stroke of the hot rod, which is to startle mankind, absorbed in worldly pursuit and to prepare the way for the mighty reaction whence the plenitude of the spiritual blessings of the millennium is to proceed. Living in a higher sphere, but near at hand, the faithful, who will have been glorified at the Advent of the Lord, will be in communion with the early saints, just as the Risen Christ was in Communion with His disciples until the ascension. The saints will not taste the dark night of seven years tribulation, for they will be exulting themselves in the joy of the Marriage Supper of the Lamb—the Great Messianic banquet.

Some years ago, while the century was still young, certain religious students of the Pyramids, devotees of pyramidology, in their study of the sepulchral Chambers of Kings, near Cairo, believed that this ancient monument placed the date of the Rapture in the month of September 1936. But throughout our study of this monumental subject, we noted on the unimpeachable authority of Jesus Himself, that we do not know when the Rapture and "catching up" and translation of the Church, His glorious body and bride will take place.

> Watch therefore; for ye know neither the day nor the hour wherein the Son of man cometh (St. Matt. 25:13).
> Watch therefore; for ye know not what hour your Lord doth come (St. Matt. 24:42).
> And take heed to yourselves, lest at any time your hearts be overcharged with . . . cares of this life, and so that day come upon you unawares (Luke 21:34).

This knowledge of the Holy Event, kept secret with the Father, will not and cannot be computed, dated through antiquity and ancient landmark, or announced by finite man nor human prophet. The believers are to be watchful and ready in prayerful expectation moment by moment.

> Therefore be ye also ready: for in such an hour as ye think not the Son of man cometh (St. Matt. 24:44).

Who are the Raptured? Parousia, or the lifting up of the saints out of the world, will embrace all true members of the redeemed Church, from Adam, the Alpha of the human race, to the Omega, to the last-hour confessor of Christ before He comes. It merits to check ourselves with the above Thessalonian passages where we are instructed that the Lord will descend from heaven with a shout, with the voice of an archangel and with the trump of God. Consider carefully the scriptural and divine order: the dead in Christ shall rise first. By "the dead in Christ" are meant all who experienced the knowledge of personal salvation through the regenerating power of the Holy Spirit and who established their spiritual status of new birth as believers in the death and resurrection of the Lord Jesus Christ (Rom. 10:9-10): be they dead saints under the old covenant times or the New Testament. Next step in the divine order, following the raising of the dead is the living believer. Such of them as are alive and remaining and ready are "caught up"; translated and carried off into life without dying at all. There will, of course, be no need of resurrection for those who are alive at Christ's Coming, for their souls and mortal bodies have not been parted. But the meaning here is the equivalent of the resurrection. It is the same change to incorruption and immortality; not from the grave indeed, but from mortal life. But, oh, there shall be a glorious transformation. When the saints are caught up to meet the Lord in the air, they shall not go as they are, with their mortal limitations of pain, disease and deformities. A mighty and miraculous change will take place and their bodies will be glorified; the whole corporeal being, refashioned to heavenly qualities and to a sublimer life than ever was dreamed before. Hosts of them were reviled, persecuted, evil spoken of with cruel mockings and scourgings and of bonds and imprisonments, while cloud of others were tormented and slain with the sword, because they were consecrated to God as His torchbearers in earthly life; because of their faith, devotion and self-sacrifice to their Lord and Saviour, they resented not, but being released forever from the death-working law in their fleshly members they counted it all joy, and were exceeding glad, sure that it was working for them a far more exceeding and eternal weight of glory and unapproachable holiness.

For our conversation is in heaven; from whence also we look for the Saviour, the Lord Jesus Christ:
Who shall change our vile body, that it may be fashioned like unto his glorious body, according to the working whereby he is able even to subdue all things unto himself (Phil. 3:20-21).

The Reverend Gerard T. Noel, in his able and full pre-millennial exposition on the "Prospects of the Christian Church," early in the nineteenth century eloquently wrote: "At the dawn of 'the day of the Lord,' 'the first resurrection' or the resurrection of the 'dead in Christ' will take place. These will awake fashioned after the glorious body of Christ; while the saints at that time living on the earth will undergo a momentous change; a change effected not through the ordinary medium of death, but of some rapid and spiritual process, which will at once assimilate them to the glorified dead, now restored to immortal life; and these saints, the dead thus revived, and the living thus changed, (and both glorified after the pattern of Christ), these saints will ascend to meet the Lord, as he approaches towards the earth, in the mingled 'glories of his Father and of the holy angels.' These saints, thus revived and changed, will form the elect church, and be presented as the glorious bride to Christ, being now 'made perfect, without spot, or wrinkle, or any such thing.' Then will the joyful hour be arrived when the marriage supper of the Lamb will be celebrated, 'because the bride shall have made herself ready.' Then will the happy and redeemed church, thus united to her Lord, prepare to reign with him on the earth, and to share his millennial glory."

In a moment these saints, weak, feeble, poor, sick and dying, who have passed through eternal revolution, shall suddenly become possessed of strength, the poor of unsearch-able riches, the sick and dying of perpetual life and the aged of unchangeable youth! All the cares and fears—the universal agony of life—shall in a moment be shaken off, never to return again. All the miseries and agitations of the earth shall shrink away from such Christians on every side, like a mist, and leave in its wake, unbroken serenity. From the mire and gloom of these dreary and pollution-poisoned climates, the watchful children of God shall pass away, to float along the amber clouds of the empyrean. From the mean and corrupt rule of corrupt governments, the believers shall be summoned to participate in the all-embracing councils of the Great King. For the saints of the Most High God shall possess the kingdom forever and ever.

These saints, Christ's hovering armies are not, however, to be silent spectators of the scene. That would be unbefitting the greatness of the moment. Their hearts are to swell with an irrepressible sense of the grandeur and glory of the Saviour's attributes and purposes, and are to breathe their fervid homage in ascriptions of might, and wisdom, and love; in bursts of adoration and joy at the redemption he has accomplished for them. What an epoch that will be to the conscious universe! What a moment to the rising dead! What a manifestation will it present of Christ's deity, of the fulness of his perfections, and of his dominion over all his works! No other display of the beauty of illimitable power and knowledge, all perfect goodness and grace, can transcend that which the instant summons of myriads and millions of mortal bodies from the ruins of death to a glorious immortal life will form. They are to be raised incorruptible and spiritual.

It is sown in corruption; it is raised in incorruption:
It is sown in dishonour; it is raised in glory: it is sown in weakness; it is raised in power:
It is sown a natural body; it is raised a spiritual body (I Cor. 15:42-44),

"How high then the office; how great the glory; how splendid the triumph of that elect and redeemed church, to whom God will give power to maintain the earth in peace; to guard it from Satanic assaults, and to uphold the claims of faith and of truth, and the joys of love in the world! Can a nobler felicity be imagined than in the very presence and under the smiles of a redeeming God, to exercise this dominion over a world once the Aceldama of the universe, but now restored to be like the Paradise of Eden?" "Blessed are the pure in heart; for they shall see God, and Blessed are the meek; for they shall inherit the earth."

Related to the work at hand and Scriptural passage above, the author humbly and reverently records here, to the glory of God, an apocalyptic experience of his own. On two different occasions during more than half a century as an ordained minister of the Gospel, I experienced vital views of Christ's Second Coming. They were not dreams, but full-orbed visions—visions in the night, indeed victorious apparitions, visible phenomena of awe, transcending all thought: distinct manifestations of the Saviour's glorified form to the bodily eye.

There was a sudden and unspeakably glorious opening in heaven above as if summoning the earth below to witness the righteousness, majesty and power of the Almighty, as in prophet Ezekiel's vision when the heaven opened as he saw visions of God. As the sun comes up behind clouds and disperses them with its bright and brilliant beams, the Lord Jesus Christ, robed in billowing and flaming colors of the rainbow, appeared against a clear sky and over a sharp-cut horizon. Fiery shapes, moving like a stream of lightning, began to appear amidst the bright dazzling clouds which came rushing down as on the wings of a whirlwind. At length it reached its destined place; it paused—then suddenly unfolding disclosed at once the Man, Christ Jesus, resplendent in all the glories of the Godhead. His presence and appearance instantly signaled a swift and supernatural movement from the watchful living on earth below, upward to heaven, for every eye saw Him. It was an absolute opposite of battle-bound paratroopers who float down from above to combat corridors on earth below. The community of Christian believers and God's saints who look for His appearing, in an ecstasy of awe, were lifted and went up in a great company as far as the eye could see; as if drawn by a mighty and miraculous magnet. As they went up, the earth began to recede, the footwear and garments dropped off from the bodies, like bronzed leaves of autumnal days, and conjoined into such an extraordinary presence of God's glory that it seemed as though the soul could no longer abide in the body. It was a transcendently glorious sight when the voice of the Omnipotent summoned the dead to arise and come forth from their graves. New terror struck the unprepared living on every side when under their very feet the earth heaved in convulsions; graves opened and the dead came forth. Meanwhile, angels gathered together the faithful servants of Christ, bearing them aloft to meet the Lord in the air where they are awarded everlasting life. The hearts of the saints were filled with love's purest joy because of the advent and appearance of the Great Captain of their salvation with his hosts around Him from the heavenly world. The Bridegroom welcomed the Bride like a traveler through the sky and midair. The vile bodies were changed and fashioned like unto His glorious body now clothed in white robes. Immortal vigor sparkled in their eyes and beauty's blush crimsoned their radiant faces; robes of glittering white are brought by attendant angels and like the fleecy drapery of the skies unfold their glorified bodies which once were gushing fountains of many tears, are now adorned with unfading crowns, that flash sweet beams of light from every pearl with glowing diadems and tiaras bright. Was it not of such experience that the veteran Apostle wrote:

Eye hath not seen, nor ear heard, neither have entered into the heart of man the things which God prepared for them that love him (I Cor. 2:9).

As for me, a spiritual experience of nearly three score years ago, I have not forgotten and I do not expect to forget. *Laudate Dominum*—praise the Lord. We shall gaze with unblanching eyes upon His glorified person and our visage shall be changed into His glorious image and likeness—the glory of the Second Life.

What the first Adam lost in the fall, the second Adam regains in Resurrection and Rapture. A miracle? Yes! And why not? Consider the water theology. In water, on which we daily depend as one of the essentials of life, there are two gases; separate them and they burn; mix them, they put fire out. Then again, out of water we have snow, fog and vapor; and all these are changes in the natural world. When we come to the thought of supernatural world, why then should we doubt and indeed be troubled over a change in the natural bodies of the living saints when they enter the realm of the supernatural world at the time of the Second Coming of Christ:

> Behold, I shew you a mystery; we shall not all sleep, but we shall all be changed,
> In a moment, in the twinkling of an eye, at the last trump; for the trumpet shall sound, and the dead shall be raised incorruptible, and we shall be changed (I Cor. 15:51-52).

With a shout which indicates command, music is played to set an army or fleet in motion. The angelic host and company of the spirits of the just are compared to a vast army, and Christ, the Captain of Salvation, by His word of command, sets it in motion, and it, in the alacrity of joyful obedience, accompanies Him to judgment.

Under the old dispensation there is a special prominence assigned to the trumpet. By it, assemblies were summoned, journeys started, feasts proclaimed. It is employed by our Lord as in the text. The voice of the trumpets is the most significant voice known to the Holy Scriptures. God Himself gave to His ancient people very special directions in the use of the trumpet. The time for the blowing of trumpets was always a time of solemnity—a time for men to bestir themselves greatly in one way or another. Trumpets proclaimed the great festivals. Trumpets were blown to call a holy convocation. Trumpets of the Jubilee were to sound in the day of atonement. Trumpets were to announce inauguration of royalty: "Behold Solomon is King over Israel." Trumpets are also associated with the manifestation of the terrible majesty and power of God. When the Almighty appeared on Mount Sinai, there was "the voice of the trumpet exceeding loud; so that all people that was in the camp trembled." Trumpets connect with the overthrow of the ungodly. It was at the blowing of the trumpets that the walls of Jericho fell down, and the city was given into the hands of Joshua. Trumpets also proclaimed the laying of the foundations of God's temple. With these facts before us we are ready to inquire into the mission and meaning of "trumpet" in connection with the apocalypse of Jesus Christ. Paul calls this "the last trump." It will call together the rejoicing saints to the heavenly Zion: like Joshua's trumpet it will be to some the signal of dismay; it will mean weal or woe according to the character of those who hear. "We shall not all sleep, but we shall all be changed," not unclothed of their bodies, but clothed upon with immortality, a kind of death and resurrection in one. Thus changed, these shall be caught up together with the others in one united and rejoicing company; "caught up" with a quick and resistless rapture as the word implies from the troubled and imperfect earth—changed as a blossom.

The meeting place—"in the air." We naturally place alongside this the ascension of Elijah or that of our Lord. In this, as in all else, He has gone before His people and pointed out for them the way. "The air" is not the atmosphere but infinite space as opposed to earth. The ancients fancied that the Milky Way is the path trod by the immortals to the palace of the King. The fable is but a distorted reflection of the truth. What it fancied, the apostle declared—a pathway in the skies on which the saints are yet to pass to meet their Lord, that He may conduct them home. "And so we shall ever be with the Lord." Less than this can never satisfy Christ's saints; more than this they cannot desire nor conceive—perfect security, sinlessness, happiness and glory.

From Greenland's icy mountains, from India's coral strand; from Africa's sunny fountains, from many ancient rivers and many plains, those who sleep in Christ will be awakened by the sound of the trumpet. From Armenia's Avarair,

> Where Noah's mighty mountain
> Uplifts its ancient head,
> And views a plain piled high with slain,
> Armenia's martyred dead

will rise to immortality. From Middle East's Der-el-zor Desert stained with the blood of countless martyrs, my own mother, brothers and sisters included, the believers whose souls have been lighted, whose natures have been ransomed by the Lamb of God, from pole to pole, to the earth's remotest corner, ocean bed and caves—the dead in Christ will hear His voice and shall arise and ascend. We who remain shall be caught up together with them in our changed bodies and shall be with our Lord and Saviour.

> All to those who have confessed
> Loved and served the Lord below,
> He will say, come near, ye blessed,
> See the kingdom I bestow;
> You forever
> Shall my love and glory know.

The Church, the ecclesia, truly called ones, like a bride is known by her "outer garment," the clothes she wears. She is wrapped up, not in the "grave clothes" of "dead works," but in garments of glory. She is not only prepared for, but anxious for the wedding day. She is wrapped up in the coming Christ. It is the message of union with the "beloved of God," that thrills her, dominates her because the Church, the bride, is Christ-centered. Her chief adornment, her first and all-consuming concern is the Lord Jesus Christ, His personal presence, His garments of holiness, His banner of love, His golden girdle of service; she hears in her heart the cry, "Even so, come, Lord Jesus!"

The betrothed, Lord's true and preeminent people, the holy martyrs, the household of faith and obedience who were affianced to him, so long waiting amid privation, persecution, contempt, shame and sorrow, now becomes a faultless and radiant Bride. The time of her marriage for the whole company of the Church of God as the Lamb's Wife has at length arrived, and the grand nuptial banquet begins: it is the union of the whole body of the saints in their spotless and shining apparel of righteousness with the personally present Christ in glory and government that declares: "Behold THY MAKER IS THY HUSBAND." The ransomed Church replies: "Lo, this is our God; we have waited for him; we will be glad and rejoice in his salvation."

Ten thousand times ten thousand
In sparkling raiment bright,
The armies of the ransomed saints
Throng up the steeps of light,
'Tis finished, all is finished,
Their fight with death and sin:
Fling open wide the golden gates,
And let the victors in.

What rush of alleluias
Fills all the earth and sky!
What ringing of a thousand harps
Bespeaks the triumph nigh!
O day, for which creation
And all its tribes were made;
O joy, for all its former woes
A thousand-fold repaid!

O then what raptured greetings
On Canaan's happy shore;

What knitting severed friendships up
Where partings are no more!
Then eyes with joy shall sparkle,
That brimmed with tears of late;
Orphans no longer fatherless,
Nor widows desolate.

Bring near Thy great salvation,
Thou Lamb for sinners slain;
Fill up the roll of Thine elect,
Then take Thy power, and reign;
Appear, Desire of nations,
Thine exiles long for home;
Show in the heaven Thy promised sign;
Thou Prince and Saviour, come.　AMEN.

IX

THE GREAT MESSIANIC TRIBULATION

"A prophetic week in Scripture is, as is well known, seven years. Sixty-nine of Daniel's prophetic weeks have been definitely and satisfactorily accounted for. 'From the going forth of the commandment'—i.e. from the decree of Artaxerxes (Neh. 2:1-8) 'to restore and build Jerusalem unto the Messiah Prince' (Dan. 9:25) was exactly 483 prophetic years, i.e. 69 weeks.' But what of the 70th week? The 70th week is still future. Between it and the past 69 weeks is a time parenthesis, an uncalendared interval, the present Christian dispensation . . . the length of which no one can tell; but at the end of it, the 70th week will begin, in which seven years' events will take place that are plainly set forth in Scripture."

Upon the translation and removal of the Church composed of the true believers from the earth, history such as the world has conceived it still continues. But the next period, the awful course of seven years will be a time of unprecedented confusion, of distress and suffering. The unrestrained power of evil lawlessness and crime will be loose and the vials of God's wrath will be poured upon the earth:

> For then shall be great tribulation, such as was not since the beginning of the world to this time, no, nor ever shall be (Matt. 24:21).

During the last three and a half of the seven years of tribulation the Antichrist will also be revealed. A man will appear in the Holy City Jerusalem endowed with miraculous powers who doeth great wonders, so that he maketh fire come down from heaven on the earth in the sight of men.

107

And he doeth great wonders, so that he maketh fire come down from heaven on the earth in the sight of men,

And deceiveth them that dwell on the earth by the means of those miracles which he had power to do in the sight of the beast; saying to them that dwell on the earth, that they should make an image to the beast, which had the wound by a sword and did live.

And he had power to give life unto the image of the beast, that the image of the beast should both speak, and cause that as many as would not worship the image of the beast should be killed.

And he causeth all, both great and small, rich and poor, free and bond, to receive a mark in their right hand, or in their foreheads:

And that no man might buy or sell, save he that had the mark, or the name of the beast, or the number of his name.

Here is wisdom. Let him that hath understanding count the number of the beast: for it is the number of a man; and his number is Six hundred three score and six (Rev. 13:13-18).

Though this man will be hailed universally as the Messiah, he is really the Antichrist, who under the influence of Satan wants power and worship for himself. He claims to be the only rightful object of human adoration; any other potency, person or some visible presence of the heavenly Kingdom about to take possession of the earth would be a thing wholly intolerable to his divine majesty.

The Antichrist will head an international dictatorship. He will be energized by Satanic power. The world has never yet seen such a man as the beast will become, when he surrenders entirely to the will of Satan. The Roman Empire is depicted as a beast in Daniel (7:7-10). This monstrosity is to be revived in the end-time of the present age, just before the Second Coming of Christ. According to Daniel (7-11), Christ will destroy the Roman beast when He returns. This can mean but one thing—namely, the predicted ten kingdoms of Caesar's

Roman Empire, as previously noted, will have to be revived and in existence, when the Lord descends from heaven. His return is announced in Daniel 7:13: "I saw in the night visions, and behold, one like the Son of man came with the clouds of heaven." Revelation 13:15 indicates that the Antichrist will cause an image to talk. He, or some other tenant of hell, claims to be animated and possessed, so as to think, speak and act only as the will of the alien spirit impels. In either case, Antichrist as a person, is an extraordinary and supernatural being. There can be no other explanation without assuming that such is the fact. The whole world will listen. It is said that a huge likeness of Mussolini was carved in stone and erected in the city of Rome. It was supposed to stand 250 feet high when completed. Dr. Bruce Corbin, the well-known prophetic lecturer, remarks that it would be possible to equip the head of this image with a radio station, so that messages could actually be broadcast through its mouth to the entire world.

The seven years fradulent covenant of the Antichrist with the Jews. The Jews, the children of the Messianic nation, yearning for their long-awaited Messiah, like a drowning man grasping eagerly at any straw that holds the slightest promise of deliverance, and with hurrahs, "Here has come our Messiah!" accept and enter into the seven years covenant with the Antichrist.

At the turn of the nineteenth century, early in March, the historian Alison wrote of a

grand Convocation of the Jews assembled in Paris, in pursuance of the commands of Napoleon, issued in the July preceding. Seventy-one doctors and chiefs of that ancient nation attended this great assembly, the first meeting of the kind which had occurred since the dispersion of the Israelites on the capture of Jerusalem. For 1700 years the children of Israel had sojourned as strangers in foreign realms; reviled, oppressed, persecuted, without a capital, without a government, without a home, far from the tombs of their forefathers, banished from the land of their ancestors; but preserving unimpaired amidst all their calamities, their traditions, their usages, their faith; exhibiting in every nation of the earth a lasting miracle to attest the verity of the Christian prophecies. On this occasion, the great Sanhedrin, or assembly published the result of their deliberations in a variety of statutes and declarations, calculated to remove from the Israelites a portion of that odium under which they had so long laboured in all the nations of Christendom; and Napoleon, in return, took them under his protection, and, under certain modifications, admitted them to the privileges of his empire.

The historian further states; "It cannot be concealed that the Jews of this Sanhedrin acknowledge the Head of the French Government as their *Deliverer* and *The Great Prince predicted in the sacred writings,* and they have shown a disposition to persuade themselves that he is the promised Messiah predicted by the ancient prophets." A noted Jewish writer, M. Jacobsohn, in his letter to the French emperor at that time, said, "I belong to that people who expected in you their Saviour, and who in you, Sire, have found him." A. M. Crouzet wrote a metrical translation of the second Psalm, making it a panegyric upon the emperor. And in the Jewish festival, on August 15, 1806, the cyphers of Napoleon and Josephine were blended with the letters expressing the name of Jehovah, and the Imperial eagle was placed over the Sacred Ark, which is said to have given offense to some, as a profanation. At the same period a pamphlet appeared in Paris, and was advertised in the *Moniteur.* Who is this [meaning the Emperor] but an Israelitish Christian? The speeches of some of the deputies to the Sanhedrin were in the highest degree adulatory to Napoleon I, and foreshadowed the eulogies which will be expressed regarding the Coming Napoleon, the Antichrist, when he shall enter into a covenant with the Jews for seven years to promote their resettlement in Palestine.

Who is this supernatural personage, Antichrist, with phenomenal and miraculous power, who with gigantic blasphemies demands worship for himself and as the recipient of all Satan's energy dictates universal policies?

This very prince of perdition incorporates himself in the government of the world, speaking through its heads, dictating its religion and its laws, controlling its trades, enforcing the worship of himself as God, cutting off those who dissent, filling the world with the worst of blasphemies, and compelling all that would live to receive the mark of allegiance to him. Although it is with the Jews only that the Antichrist will confirm the covenant for one week, yet ultimately the ten kings of the Roman earth will join together in giving their kingdoms to him until the words of God shall be fulfilled (Rev. 17:12, 13). All existing nations on the prophetic earth shall have organically conjoined themselves with him as the representative of all authority and power, "and all that dwell upon the earth shall worship him." As to his origin, he is repeatedly described as "the Beast that cometh up out of the abyss"; the evil supernatural underworld, the abode of lost spirits, otherwise called hell. Ordinary men do not come from such an extraordinary world of demons. The one who hails from that region must be either a dead man brought up again from the dead, or some evil spirit which takes possession of a living man. Many of the early Christians believed and taught that Emperor Nero is the Antichrist, and that he will return again to the earth, get possession of its empire, and enact all that is affirmed of the "Man of Sin."

Victorinus, one of the old Church Fathers, says: "Nero will be raised from the dead, appear again at Rome, persecute the Church once more, and finally be destroyed by the Messiah coming in His glory."

Lucius Lanctantius, a Christian author of the fourth century, holds to the same view, "Nero will come, the precursor

111

and forerunner of the Devil, coming to lay waste."

Another Church Father, Sulpicius Severus wrote: "Nero, the beast of men and even of monsters, was well worthy of being the first persecutor; I know not whether he may be the last, since it is the current opinion of many that he is yet to come as Antichrist."

Finally, the more celebrated Church Father, Augustine, says: "What means the declaration, that the mystery of iniquity doth already work? Some suppose it to be spoken of the Roman Emperor, and therefore Paul did not speak in plain words, although he always expected that what he says should be understood as applying to Nero, whose doings already appeared like those of Antichrist. Hence it was that some suppose that he would rise from the dead as Antichrist."

The historic Jewish rebellion in the autumn of 67 under the commander-in-chief, Josephus of Galilee, was consummated in the destruction of Jerusalem by General Titus, an appointee of Emperor Nero. It is recorded in history that, after the capture of the city, his soldiers wanted to crown Titus as conqueror. But he modestly refused the honor, alleging that he was but an instrument in the hand of heaven—which had so manifestly declared its wrath against that city of the Jews.

Dean Farrar (referring to the temple in the city) speaks of the corpses lying in piles and mounds on the very altar slopes; the fires feeding luxuriously on cedar work overlaid with gold; friend and foe trampled to death on the gleaming mosaics in promiscuous carnage: priests, swollen with hunger, leaping madly into the devouring flames:—till at last those flames had done their work, and what had been the Temple of Jerusalem, the beautiful and holy House of God, was a heap of ghastly ruin, where the burning embers were half-slaked in pools of gore."

When, in the following spring the suppression of the zealots, fanatics and angry rebels resumed in Judea, in the midst of fighting, Nero committed suicide. Nero in his lifetime boasted that every nation of the earth except the Jews adored and worshipped him. Early in the summer of 66 A.D. the Partian Prince Tiridates came to Italy and kneeling before Nero said to him: "You are my God, and I come to adore you as I adore the sun. My destiny is to be determined by your supreme will."

To which Nero replied; "I will make you King of Armenia, that the whole universe may know it belongs to me to give or take away crowns." Significantly, Tiridates was the first king in the world to adopt Christianity as the national religion in Armenia in 301 A.D.

B. W. Newton, a distinguished prophetic student, in his *Prospects of the Ten Kingdoms,* written in the mid-nineteenth century, says: "The 8th Chapter of Daniel reveals that Antichrist will spring from that part of the Roman Empire which the Romans gained from the successors of Alexander the Great."

That Antichrist is to arise as a Little Horn from the Eastern part of the Roman Empire, and from one of the four kingdoms, Greece, Egypt, Syria, or Thrace, is rendered unquestionable by Daniel viii. But, seeing that in the eleventh chapter he is mentioned as conflicting with the king of the north (i.e., the king of Syria), and also with the king of the south (i.e., the king of Egypt), it is plain that he does not arise either from Egypt or Syria. He must therefore, arise either from Greece from the districts immediately contiguous to Constantinople (ancient Thrace). It is true that if he arose from the latter, or indeed from either of the four, he would be esteemed Greek in origin, because all the four were divisions of the Greek empire; but it seems far more probable that Greece proper will be the place of his rise (as a Horn or monarch). He is described as 'Waxing great towards the south and towards the east, and towards the pleasant land'; that is, towards Egypt, Syria and Palestine—a description that would geographically suit the position of one who was supposed to be in Greece.

While in Christian tradition Nero appears to the Church Fathers as the mystic Antichrist because he displayed the attributes of "monster of wickedness" who was destined to come once again to torment the saints as the very incarnation of iniquity; they had no knowledge of Sultan Abdul Hamid, the persecuting despot, the "bloody assassin" and Turkish woe, who paid the price all tyrants and despots must pay. Himself obsessed by the terror of assassination, and learning of a threat upon his life by the insurgents and revolutionists, Hamid withdrew into the fortified seclusion of Yildiz Palace, and upon his inevitable capitulation was exiled to Magnesia in Asia Minor where he died the death of an outcast. The explosion came. A national declaration based on the declaration of the French Revolution: (*L'homme et du citoyen*), the right of every citizen to *Liberty, Equality* and *Security* was made by the young Turks, deposers of the sultan. The declaration was a document of prophetic importance, expressing the unconquerable hope of all citizens, especially the Armenians; who suffered so long under a government of unbearable misrule. But the decisive act of revolutionary drama, instead of unfolding an era, nurtured by nobility by carrying out the spirit of the declaration, ushered in a sinister warlord dictatorship by the ferocious Committee of Union and Progress headed by historical villains, Enver Bey, the prime minister, and by the murderous Minister of the Interior, Talaat Pasha, respectively the precursors of Hitler and Adolf Eichmann, perpetrators of the horrors and brutality of the Nazi regime. Talaat, the terrible Turk, taking advantage of an international carnage and horrendous political confusion and chaos, telegraphed to every seat of government throughout the land an adamant range of regulations, ordering the deportation and destruction of three million civilian Armenian Christians; an atrocious event that constructed the anatomy and ultimate horror of THE FIRST

114

GENOCIDE OF THE 20th CENTURY: A WOUND THAT WILL NOT HEAL!

This atrocious wickedness produced such evil consequences of rousing the lower orders by the most savage, rapacious and lawless of the people, that the peaceable and inoffensive citizens wept and suffered in silence; terror and sword crushed every attempt and extremity of grief, subdued even the firmest hearts. In despair at effecting any alleviation of the far-flung persecution and massacre which universally prevailed, the suffering Armenians sought to forget their sorrow in the delirium of the reign of terror and death! Many were barbarously mangled, and left by the wayside to perish, scores were hanged, and thousands were buried alive in the sands of Der-el-zor Desert, southeast of Aleppo. Such heinous crimes and diabolical acts of relentless massacres, inhuman brutality, degradation of women—a numb saturnalia of lust, crimes and atrocity and wholesale extermination of a subject race—a race that high ranking international observers have spoken of as "possessors of the highest culture, civilization and indestructible spirituality in Asia Minor" brands Talaat as one of the greatest criminals, not only of the twentieth century, but of all human history. Victor Hugo's bitter litany and searing indictment: "The Turk has trodden this land, all is ruins!" stands at once as a fitting epitaph to the Turkish national character—a character that profaned through these acts the basic respect for human beings. The Armenians died all the deaths of the earth, the death of all ages, when Talaat in Hitlerian style and scale built bridges of the atrociously massacred and starved men, women and innocent children for their artillery wheels—the total ultimate in a sinister atmosphere of death and terror.

For nearly half a thousand years, the benighted Turk, condemned already at the bar of God and of civilization, has been the odious scourge, wreaking his wicked will upon Christian subjects: an oppressive oligarchy avowedly Antichristian. The ancient Church Fathers may nominate NERO, a tenant of the abyss; B. W. Newton may point to Hellenic Greece and to the Macedonian kingdom embracing Thrace, i.e. European Turkey, south of Balkans; other erudite prophetic scholars may look elsewhere as the country of the Antichrist's origin; but as for me, humbly now, I take the crown from off the head of NERO as a monster of horror and Beast of hideous crimes against the saints, and place it on the head of Thomas Carlyle's "THE UNSPEAKABLE TURK!"

Whatever the real identity of this mysterious character of iniquity, whichever country or region he springs from in this present world of the living, or returns from the abode of the dead, as an incarnation of the Devil, he is at once the consummate antagonist of everything Divine. He is anti-God, anti-Christ, and anti-Spirit, antagonizing each Person of the adorable Holy Trinity on their claims, usurping their honours, putting himself into their place and abolishing all worship, taking the lead in the administration upon earth, to the great wonder and astonishment of the whole world. The Antichrist, the false god, hates and blasphemes the Only True God and bitterly opposes the holy character of God, because he knows God is determined to execute wrath and judgment against him and against all evildoers.

Consider now, what is the significance of Antichrist's league with a small nation like Israel? No larger than Rhode Island, Palestine (or Israel) is now a small country, only a tiny spot on the earth's surface, a narrow streak. It is possible to drive comfortably in a single day around its borders: 150 miles from north to south, 25 miles across at its narrowest point) 9500 square miles. Though the present state of Israel is smaller by a fifth, the astounding geographical change of the Six Days War of 1967 brought back, in part at least, the old kingdoms of the renowned kings David and Solomon, which were Israel's from the beginning.

In our earlier exposition under the "Jewish Sign" we gave the Scriptural and authoritative information of the extent and real boundaries of God's Palestine, embracing the Abrahamic covenant confirmed and made everlasting by El Shaddai, Almighty God, and that Israel owns this land.

> In the same day the Lord made a covenant with Abram, saying, Unto thy seed have I given this land, from the river of Egypt unto the great river, the river Euphrates: (Gen. 15:18),
>
> And I will give unto thee, and to thy seed after thee, the land wherein thou art a stranger, all the land of Canaan, for an everlasting possession; and I will be their God (Gen. 17:8).
>
> I will set thy bounds from the Red Sea, even unto the Sea of the Philistines, and from the desert unto the river (Ex. 23:31).

Here is the incontestable record that the title of the land is given to Abraham and his seed, and is to be an everlasting possession for them (I Chron. 18:3). In the light of these Holy Scriptures, intangible wonder that Israel, by regaining the dominion of David and Solomon from the Nile in the south unto the great river Euphrates in the north, looks ahead to becoming a mighty nation, possessing the major wealth of this planet with power and prestige. This is the future that his eminence, Antichrist, eyes in being in league with Israel: to establish his empire and extend his antichristian apostasy.

Concerning a further comment on Antichrist, while he is better known as the "Man of Sin" or the "Son of Perdition," there is another aspect of him that should receive consideration. Incredible as it may seem, he will be a representative of peace, seeking to settle the perplexing and poignant problems of the world. This is why Israel will be attracted to him, though he is subject to, mainly Satan, who offers him a religious ally in the Person of a False Prophet, posing as the spiritual leader of the world. The False Prophet, then, shall direct the worship of the world toward the Antichrist, who performs miracles by calling fire out of heaven. Then will occur THE ABOMINATION OF DESOLATION.

> When ye therefore shall see the abomination of desolation, spoken of by Daniel the prophet, stand in the holy place, whoso readeth, let him understand: (St. Matt. 24:15).
>
> Who opposeth and exalteth himself above all that is called God, or that is worshipped; so that he as God sitteth in the temple of God, shewing himself that he is God (II Thess. 2:4).

Israel, who by their conquest of Old Jerusalem in June 1967, have taken David's capital, will have rebuilt the temple while still in covenant with the Antichrist—who will be visited by the False Prophet who brings with him a golden image of the Antichrist into Jerusalem, such as Nebuchadnezzar made—and wheels it into the temple. Into this image the vagabond angel will enter, emitting voices and oracles. The Lord Jesus had this event in mind in the above passage when He spoke of "the abomination of desolation," that of the image being taken into God's temple, more than the destruction of Jerusalem by the Roman General Titus in 70 A.D. This image will be given the power of human speech. During the New York World's Fair 1964-1965, the late Walt Disney created a life-sized figure that looked, acted and spoke like Abraham Lincoln. This image of Antichrist will speak and through its manmade metallic mouth, supernaturally giving forth out of the dead metal oracles and commands, and all the savants of the time will stand in homage to this deity. Failure to pay adoration to the image is punishable by death! The world will wonder after it and will become devil worshippers. Here the Jews will discover that this Messiah had feet of clay and the pretender was a liar and deceiver and that they were seriously in error, for it is written in the law of the land:

> Ye shall make you no idols nor graven image, neither rear you up a standing image, neither shall ye set up any image of stone in your land, to bow down unto it: For I am the LORD your God (Lev. 26:1).

118

It is said that King Antiochus IV of Syria (called Epiphanes), when he seized Jerusalem in 170 B.C., plundered, profaned and desecrated the Jewish temple by offering a sow upon the altar and erecting an altar to Jupiter. Polybius, the contemporary Greek historian, observed that for Antiochus IV, plundering temples was his specialty, who had "despoiled most sanctuaries." This "desolation" is considered the type of the final "abomination of desolation" (Matt. 24:15).

The people were forbidden to worship in the temple and were compelled to eat the flesh of swine. A great massacre of 40,000 Jews followed. Women and children were sold into slavery. Temple worship was abandoned. The worship of Olympian Zeus, too, was set up in the temple of Yahweh. Jewish religion was forbidden. For taking part in any Jewish religious ceremonies—the traditional sacrifices, the Sabbath, or circumcision, the penalty was death. The Holy Scriptures were destroyed. By these shattering blows and thoroughgoing religious persecutions, Antiochus the monster, a type of Antichrist, did his utmost to obliterate the Jewish religion and hoped to crush and destroy the faith of Israel—the people of God. While devising new and more formidable plans for the destruction of the Jews, he, like Herod, died of a loathesome disease.

When the Jews see the image of the Antichrist in the temple at Jerusalem showing himself that he is God and with people prostrate before it they rebel against him. They will pluck up real courage to cast out of their temple his image which will have stood there for 1290 days (Dan. 12:11). So on the expiration of three and one half years or 42 months, as clearly predicted by Daniel and in Revelation, having been revealed in his true character as the Man of Sin, he breaks his covenant with the Jews, stops the daily sacrifice which has been resumed, and has his own image set up in the Holy place and, an avowed infidel denying all the doctrines of the Church of God, demands that he in his open blasphemy be worshipped as God.

It is upon this break that the Man of Sin, the personal Antichrist, unleashes the most terrible persecution of unequalled violence and severity of the Jews that the world has ever witnessed. The lightnings and the thunder of Satan's fury will fall around Israel's head (St. Matt. 24:19-21). Many Jews will be destroyed. Others will flee in greater terror than ever they fled from the machine-gun fire and lethal gas chambers of Adolph Hitler. The flight will bring them east across the Allenby Bridge into Transjordania, down the desert treks into the impenetrable Mount Seir, whose chief city was Sela, now called Petra, the Rose Red and beautiful Rainbow City in the mountainous land of Edom between the Dead Sea and the Gulf of Akabah: a rocky ridge in the center of which is Mount Hor, where Aaron the high priest of the Israelites died and was buried. *Mount Seir:* Precipitous cliffs of pink and mauve granite thrust their way upward to the blue sky. Between them sparkle slopes and gorges of pale amber and fiery red bands of feldspar. It is as if all the color and beauty of a garden had been poured into this wild serrated symphony in stone at the margin of the wilderness. Esau, of Biblical fame, who despised his birthright, once lived in this most beautiful city of the world, with its palaces carved like beautiful cameos out of rose red, rainbow-hued and lemon-colored stones, and his family reigned as dukes and kings (Gen. 36:15-43). Set on a rock and rocky fastness, a natural fortress nearly 2500 feet high, arising with sudden and sheer height from the surrounding desert south of Jerusalem, this mysterious and desolate city, once a city of great wealth and luxury which was inhabited by more than 250,000 people, will be a hiding place during the Great Tribulation. In this strange place of desolate beauty, there are caves and caverns of exquisite excellence, enough to accomodate 100,000 refugees in comfort.

Joseph Hoffman Cohn, a noted Jewish missioner, in his brochure, *The Man from Petra,* relates a conversation with W. E. Blackstone, an honored saint, who more than any other Bible student at the beginning of the century brought the

Second Coming of Christ to the attention and consciousness of the Church. Mr. Cohn, whom the writer had the privilege of hearing as a theological student, referring to the author of *Jesus is Coming,* says this:

> He told me something that astounded me. He said that he had just sent $8,000 to a Jewish missionary in Palestine, and that that Jewish missionary had made up a caravan of donkeys and camels and had accrued thousands of Gospel tracts, New Testaments, and Gospels, clear down through the desert of Transjordania and up into the mountain height of Petra. And there he had distributed these New Testaments and tracts in small packages, in the caves and in the empty houses, to bide the time when the refugee Israelites will flee there for escape from the Antichrist. Then they will find these New Testaments and they will understand what is going on, and what their Messiah is doing for their deliverance! I must confess that I had a feeling of astonishment, and I thought within myself that this was surely something fantastic. But here was a man known to be sober in judgment, a good Bible student, and he had taken of his own money the sum of $8,000 to make an investment of this sort. Who then was I to gainsay?

So everything is ready and waiting, including thousands of Bibles and New Testaments in the Hebrew language for Tribulation-torn Israel to read and come to understand who indeed their true Messiah really is.

The Great Tribulation period will be a time of mighty Spiritual Revival and Salvation through the preaching mission of Moses and Elijah—God's two witnesses, who were with Christ at the time of His transfiguration on the Holy Mount. The elect Jews shall be saved during this time, also innumerable multitudes of Gentiles.

121

And I will give power unto my two witnesses, and they shall prophesy a thousand two hundred and three score days, clothed in sackcloth.

These are the two olive trees, and the two candlesticks standing before the God of the earth.

And if any men will hurt them, fire proceedeth out of their mouth, and devoureth their enemies: and if any man will hurt them, he must in this manner be killed.

These have power to shut heaven, that it rain not in the days of their prophecy: and have power over waters to turn them to blood, and to smite the earth with all plagues, as often as they will.

And when they shall have finished their testimony, the beast that ascendeth out of the bottomless pit shall make war against them, and shall overcome them, and kill them.

And their dead bodies shall lie in the street of the great city, which spiritually is called Sodom and Egypt, where also our Lord was crucified.

And they of the people and kindreds and tongues and nations shall see their dead bodies three days and an half, and shall not suffer their dead bodies to be put in graves.

And they that dwell upon the earth shall rejoice over them, and make merry, and shall send gifts one to another; because these two prophets tormented them that dwelt on the earth.

And after three days and an half the Spirit of life from God entered into them, and they stood upon their feet; and great fear fell upon them which saw them.

And they heard a great voice from heaven saying unto them, Come up hither. And they ascended up to heaven in a cloud; and their enemies beheld them.

And the same hour was there a great earthquake, and the tenth part of the city fell, and in the earthquake were slain of men seven thousand: and the remnant were affrighted, and gave glory to the God of heaven (Rev. 11:3-13).

And I heard the number of them which were sealed: and there were sealed an hundred and forty and four thousand of all the tribes of the children of Israel (Rev. 7:4-8).

After this I beheld, and, lo, a great multitude, which no man could number, of all nations, and kindreds, and people, and tongues, stood before the throne, and before the Lamb, clothed with white robes, and palms in their hands;

And cried with a loud voice, saying, Salvation to our God which sitteth upon the throne, and unto the Lamb.

And all the angels stood round about the throne, and about the elders and the four beasts, and fell before the throne on their faces, and worshipped God,

Saying, Amen: Blessing, and glory, and wisdom, and thanksgiving, and honour, and power, and might, be unto our God forever and ever. Amen.

And one of the elders answered, saying unto me, What are these which are arrayed in white robes? and whence came they?

And I said unto him, Sir, thou knowest. And he said to me, These are they which came out of great tribulation, and have washed their robes, and made them white in the blood of the Lamb (Rev. 7:9-14).

In the spirit of rightly dividing the word of truth, it is highly important to observe and differentiate between two 144,000's: the one in the seventh chapter, the other 144,000 on "Mount Zion" recorded in the fourteenth chapter, who are called "the firstfruits unto God" (Rev. 14:4). The 144,000 in the seventh chapter are *totally different* from the 144,000 on Mount Zion in the fourteenth chapter. The 144,000 in the seventh chapter are those who were converted and sealed during the great tribulation on earth, while the Mount Zion 144,000 in the fourteenth chapter 144,000 are mostly Gentiles, and not at all city of the living God, the heavenly Jerusalem (Heb. 12:22)." Once again, the 144,000 of the seventh chapter who came out of the great Tribulation are distinctly Jews, whereas the fourteenth chapter 144,000 are mostly Gentiles, and not at all described as being Jews, but are called the *firstfruits*—a term in no wise applicable to Israelites. Finally, the fourteenth chapter 144,000 are called *a* and not *the* 144,000, and this shows they are not the same as the previously mentioned seventh chapter 144,000, because in Revelation it is an invariable rule that, if the same object is mentioned a second time it always has the definite article *the* prefixed to it.

X
PLANET'S FINAL BATTLE—ARMAGEDDON

The cosmic event that ushers in the end of the Great Tribulation is ARMAGEDDON, the popular cognomen attached to the GREAT BATTLE of all time. The name "Harmageddon" is from the Hebrew root, meaning to cut off, to slay; and the Valley of Megiddo which belts across the middle of the Holy Land from the Mediterranean to the River Jordan has ever been a place of slaughter. From the long standing scriptural identification and Bible prophecy the conflict is called "The Battle of that great day of God Almighty" (Rev. 16:14). Armageddon has been one of God's great battlegrounds of the Old Testament between theocracy and its enemies of false deity claiming for themselves divine authority where the armies of the wicked and apostate world have been judged. The dark and ominous clouds of mortal conflict are again hanging low over that perimeter of the planet, that might easily be the beginning of the approaching Armageddon. As poignantly portrayed in the Messianic prophecy of Ezekiel (38) the armies of the Northern Confederacy, joined by "the Kings of the East," horses and horsemen, clothed with bewildering array of armours, and with great company and a mighty army with shields, all of them their faces set, with brandishing swords; they come. They come down "like a storm" over the mountains: "Like a cloud to cover the Land, multitudes, multitudes, in the valley of decision": armies on armies, hosts on hosts in league with the Antichrist who promises to mankind a new golden age under his rule; without God when they plunder the Holy City. The kings and captains, mighty men of valor and drilled legions of all nations are there; all gathered into one great pen of

125

slaughter. The divine taunt thus expressed reflects the character of the proceedings which it scorns. The nations are on fire with rage. Why?

> Why do the nations rage, and the people imagine a vain thing?
> The kings of the earth set themselves, and the rulers take counsel together, against the LORD, and against his anointed, saying,
> Let us break away their bands asunder, and cast away their cords from us.
> He that sitteth in the heavens shall laugh; the Lord shall have them in derision (Ps. 2:1-4).

Where, then, is Armageddon? Armageddon or Megiddo was situated in the great plain of the tribe of Issachar, famous for a double slaughter, first of the Canaanites (Judges 5:19) and again of the Israelites (II Kings 23:29). In the apocalypse it signifies the place where the kings opposing the Lord Jesus Christ are to be destroyed with a slaughter like that which Canaanites or the Israelites had experienced of old.

Toward the north hills of Galilee, with the historic town of Nazareth, the boyhood home of Jesus Christ (visited by the author), sweeping upward, tinted a delicate blue and far to the right, the somber summit of Mount Tabor bars the view into the deep cleft of the Jordan Valley. Nothing in this fertile valley, this friendly countryside surrounded by gentle lines of hills, suggests that this narrow tip of land was for many centuries the scene of mighty battles and will be the theatre of Armageddon, the most momentous and decisive conflict of history. Hardly a flower blooms there but has in its veins the inherited blood of parent flowers that drank the crimson streak of contending armies. Hardly a foot of that triangular plain that has not at some time been gullied with war chariots or trampled with hoofs of charging cavalry. Tabor, Gilboa and Carmel have heard the crash and felt the shock of mighty

126

hosts, and the stream Kishon has oft run red with blood of many thousands. In 1500 B.C. Pharaoh Tutmose III, riding in a "golded chariot," led his army through a narrow pass into the plain of Jezreel and attacked the Canaanites, who fled in complete disorder to Megiddo. On this same plain the Israelites under the heroic and inspiring leadership of Judge Deborah, Israel's Joan of Arc, and Captain Barak smashed the supremacy of King Jabin the Canaanite and his 900 chariots of iron led by Commander Sisera. Whether there was a shower of meteors, or a storm of hailstones, the Scriptures tell us that, "the stars in their courses fought against Sisera." Gideon, the hewer and valiant warrior, an appointee of the Almighty with his select band of 300 men with pitchers and lamps, with burning torches—the fire bombs of the ancient world—surprised the plundering and camel-borne nomads from Midian and delivered Israel. Ahab triumphed over Syrian Benhadad, and King Josiah, on his way to Mesopotamia, put an end to the invasion of the armed might of Egypt and Pharaoh Necho. There the ruddy son of Jesse the Bethlehemite met and slew the mighty Goliath of the Philistines who defied the armies of the living God. Here on the heights of Gilboa King Saul and Jonathan, father and son, found their death as they fought their last battle with the Philistines. One would imagine that the winds on the hills of Gilboa must have moaned the solemn requiem: "The Dead March in Saul," and his gallant son—Jonathan. Romans fought under Gabinius and Vespasian. Ruins mark the site of the Frankish castle of Faba which the Knights of Saint John and Templars occupied during the Crusades in the battle between the Christians of Western Europe and the Mohammedans of Eastern Europe, until Ayyubite Saladin, sultan of Egypt drove them off the plain after a frightful massacre.

On April 16, 1799, there was a battle here between the Turks of the Ottoman Empire and the French. With only 1500 men, Kleber, the French general, held 25,000 of the enemy at bay. The French fought like heroes from sunrise until noon.

Then over the ridge to the rescue charged a troop of 600 mounted men. The officer at their head was called Napoleon Bonaparte. After the victorious battle of Tabor, Napoleon rode up into the hills of Galilee and ate his supper in Nazareth. In 1918, British cavalry under Field Marshall Lord Allenby swept through the same pass as did Tutmose III of Egypt, and destroyed the Turkish army which was encamped on the plain. The Waterloo of despotism, the Hastings of freedom, were fought and found on Esdraeldon. It was on that plain that Jehu fought the battle which changed the fate of Israel, and because of the revolution which it wrought among the eastern nations, turned the history-current of the then known world. On this plain Babylon and Ninevah saw the beginning of their doom.

However peaceful, green as a pavement of emeralds, rich with its gleams of vivid sunlight and purpling shadows which floated over it from the clouds of the latter rain, it has been for centuries a battlefield of the nations. Pharaohs and Ptolemies, Emirs and Arsacids, judges and consuls have all contended for the mastery of that smiling tract. It has glittered with the lances of Amalakites; it has trembled under the chariot wheels of Sosastries; it has echoed the twanging bow-strings of Sennacherib; it has been trodden by the phalanxes of Macedonia; it has clashed with the broad swords of Rome; and with the thunder of artillery of England and France; it was destined hereafter to ring with the frenzied and furious battle-cry, "Deus Vult!"—God wills—of the Christain Crusaders. Out of every nation under heaven warriors have pitched their tents upon the great plain of Esdraeldon of the tribes of Issachar and have beheld their banners wet with the dews of notable mountains, Tabor and Hermon. Here the mighty Hermon thrusts its slopes 10,000 feet into the heavens above the flat and verdant plain. From the side of this famous mountain ridge, to the south, gushes the source of the River Jordan. Towering over both Syria and Palestine and visible from afar it seems to have been placed there by the Creator of nature as a gigantic and "ancient landmark" between them. Even in the blazing heat of Eastern summer, Hermon's peak remains covered and crowned with snow like the headdress and white turban of an Arabian emir. In that plain of Jezreel, Europe and Asia, Judaism and paganism, barbarism and civilization, the Old and New Covenant, the history of the past and the hopes of the present all meet. No scene of deeper significance for the destiny of humanity has ever existed upon this terrestrial plain than the ancient hill and valley of Megiddo, west of Jordan in the plain of Jezreel, the appointed place for the great battle—a battle without a tomorrow. Intangible wonder that here should be the seat of the winepress for the final crushing of the mighty of last evil days by the Saviour whose glory covers the earth. In the midst of the battle when the verdant plains become a Red Sea of blood from Bozrah to Esdraelon, there will suddenly flash forth with the vividness of a sheet of lightning, the shining brilliancy of the cortege of the Son of Man. They shall see the Son of Man coming in the clouds of heaven with power and great glory. It is the Mount of Messiah's Victory. The King of glory shall revenge Himself of His enemies (Isaiah 29:6), destined to the terrors of judgment. The prophet Isaiah speaking on the Judgment Day of the Lord at Armageddon spells out the awesome command to the assembled nations.

> Come near, ye nations, to hear; and hearken, ye people: let the earth hear, and all that is therein; the world, and all the things that come forth of it.
> For the indignation of the LORD is upon all nations, and his fury upon all their armies: he hath utterly destroyed them, he hath delivered them to the slaughter.
> Their slain also shall be cast out, and their stink shall come up out of their carcasses, and the mountains shall be melted with their blood.
> For my sword shall be bathed in heaven. . . .
> The sword of the LORD is filled with blood. . . . for the LORD hath a sacrifice in Bozrah, and a great slaughter in the land of Idumea.

129

For it is the day of the LORD's vengeance and the year of recompences for the controversy of Zion (Isaiah 34:1-3, 5, 6, 8).

These plains are yet to be the locality of the battle of Armageddon, in which more lives shall be lost, more blood shall be shed, and more startling horrors witnessed than have ever been known. The three miracle-working spirits of demons will have gathered the kings of the earth, with the flower of their armies to this famous battlefield. The primary purpose of so vast a concourse of military forces will be, as portrayed in the above prophetic Scripture, to engage in conflict with the Jews alone or with their divine Messiah, whose expected advent has been widely heralded. In either case the expedition will ultimately resolve itself into an open and avowed war on the part of the assembled armies against the coming King of Kings and Lord of Lords. "These shall make war with the Lamb, and the Lamb shall overcome them." "And I saw the beast, and the kings of the earth, and their armies, gathered together to make war against him [Christ] that sat on the horse, and against his army" (Rev. 17:14, 19:19).

The Lord Jesus Christ, with the invincible armies of heaven will appear from heaven to a rocking, shuddering and blood-stained earth—a river of human blood up to the bridles of the horses in depth.

An eminent expositor at the turn of the century added this to the apocalyptic account before us. "When the Romans destroyed Jerusalem, so great was the blood-shed," that Flavius Josephus, the Jewish historian and military commander says, "the whole city ran down with the blood to such a degree that the fires of many of the houses were quenched by it." "When Sylla took Athens," Plutarch says, "the blood that was shed in the marketplace alone covered all the ceramicus as far as Dipylus, and some testify that it ran through the gates and overflowed the suburbs."

What Apostle John, the exiled saint in the Island of Patmos saw and described is "the great wine-press of the wrath of God." It is the last great consummate act of destruction which is to end this present world. The masses on whom it is executed are the kings of the earth and of the whole world, and their armies stationed in a line from Bozrah in Edom to Esdraelon in Galilee.

> Our God shall come, and shall not keep silence: a fire shall devour before him, and it shall be very tempestuous round about him.
> He shall call to the heavens from above, and to the earth, that he may judge his people.
> Gather my saints together unto me; those that have made a covenant with me by sacrifice.
> And the heavens shall declare his righteousness: for God is judge himself (Ps. 50:3-6).

The Lord Jesus Christ will appear from heaven and at His coming in great glory will deliver the children of the Messianic nation besieged by the Gentile world powers who are gathered against Jerusalem to battle:

> Then shall the Lord go forth, and fight against those nations, as when he fought in the day of battle (Zech. 14:3).

It is the battle of the great day of God Almighty. It is the coming forth of the powers of eternity to take possession of the earth. It finds all the confederate kingdoms of man mustered in rebellion against the anointed and rightful sovereign of the earth. To the Church Jesus Christ is the High Priest, with girdle and ephod, stars and lamps, the minister of righteousness unto salvation. To the world in armed rebellion He is the mounted Warrior, the minister of righteousness unto destruction; but in both and always "Jesus Christ the Righteous." When the armed mob came forth against Him in

131

Gethsemane, He spoke to them, "I am he"; they went backward, and fell on the ground. If so mild an utterance prostrated his enemies then, what will it be when he girds and crowns himself for the "Battle of the great day of God Almighty"—when he cometh with all the cavalcade of heaven to tread the winepress of the fierceness of Jehovah's wrath? It was in anticipation of this that the Psalmist was moved to sing: "Gird thy sword upon thy thigh, O most Mighty, with thy glory and thy majesty" (Ps. 45:3). When the Lord Jesus is revealed from heaven, in flaming fire taking vengeance upon them that know not God and that obey not the Gospel, but have confederated with Hell to hold it even against the forces of Omnipotence, he does not come alone. His bride is with him now. Even before the flood, Enoch prophesied of this epiphany of the promised One, "Behold the Lord cometh with ten thousand of his saints to execute judgment upon all" (Jude 14, 15).

The beauteous forms of radiant angels soaring upward with the elect safely carried in their powerful grasp will appear rapidly winging their way through the gleaming skies: they will rifle this terrestrial casket of all the elect, who are its jewels: they will leave it without a solitary believing Christian, and moral "darkness will cover the earth, and gross darkness the people." Instead of being led by these circumstances to repent and fear God and work righteousness, the imperial Antichrist will now become more steeled in the desperate resolve to enter into mortal combat with the approaching armies of heaven, or to perish in the attempt. Behind him will surge a turbulent crew of demoralized desperadoes, abandoned adventurers, sullen conscripts, and camp followers, eager for plunder, with every variety of military costume, national banner, and weapon of war. No commander-in-chief was ever placed at the head of a larger and more heterogeneous assemblage than this. It will be a revival of the Crusades on a wider and more destructive scale. Like the herd of swine which ran violently down a steep place into the sea,

132

and were choked in its waters; so will this countless concourse of warriors from Europe, Asia, Africa, and America following the latter-day Pharaoh, whose heart will now be incurably hardened, convergently rush onward to the Red Sea of Armageddon, to be engulfed within its vortex. Then truly it will have come to pass that

> the heathen rage, and the people imagine a vain thing; the kings of the earth set themselves, and the rulers take counsel together, against the Lord, and against his Anointed, saying, Let us break their bands asunder, and cast away their cords from us. But HE that sitteth in the heavens shall laugh, the Lord shall have them in derision. Then shall he speak to them in his wrath, and vex them in his sore displeasure.

Never before was there such combination of forces, natural and supernatural, directed with such consummate skill, or animated with so daring and resolved spirit of Antichrist—a declaration of war against His Omnipotence. But the Almighty laughs! Antichrist has taught the nations and their armies under his rule to curse God and die. So, unchanged by all the terribleness of an oncoming perdition, although aching with all the truths, when God Himself had wept, they were too ignorant to weep and pray: "Come and befriend us; we have need of you"; their last words were curses and their last breath was blasphemy.

The sunset of the nations is here. The hands of the cosmic clock are approaching. Christianity has nearly 2000 years on its shoulders. The nations in their creative impulse are about exhausted; they have fulfilled their task and the time is drawing near for them to step off the stage of history by the coming of Christ to establish His Kingdom on earth.

General Douglas MacArthur, one of the central figures of military history, a most decorated hero whose name spells large in the annals of time, himself wove Armageddon into his brilliant vocabulary and authentic reminiscences. "If we do not now devise some greater and more equitable system, Armageddon will be at our door. The problem is basically theological and involves a spiritual recrudescence and improvement of human character that will synchronize with our almost matchless advances in science, art, literature and all material and cultural developments of the past two thousand years. *It must be of the spirit if we are to save the flesh."* As this Supreme Commander's and military strategist's legendary promise, *"I shall return,"* became the hope of the Philipine people and their national liberation, so the Second Coming of Jesus Christ in confirmation of His comforting and sovereign promise, *"I will come again,"* is the blessed hope of the people and cosmic purpose of God, the Church and the world!

XI

EPIPHANEIA—REVELATION

Immediately after the tribulation of those days shall the sun be darkened, and the moon shall not give her light, and the stars shall fall from heaven, and the powers of the heavens shall be shaken (St. Matt. 24:29).

And his feet shall stand in that day upon the mount of Olives, which is before Jerusalem on the east, and the mount of Olives shall cleave in the midst thereof toward the east and toward the west, and there shall be a very great valley; and half of the mountain shall move toward the north, and half of it toward the south (Zech. 14:4).

Behold, he cometh with clouds; and every eye shall see him, and they also which pierced him; and all kindreds of the earth shall wail because of him. Even so, Amen (Rev. 1:7).

This is the revelation of our Lord Jesus Christ; the lightning-flash which lays bare to public gaze the naked truth about the world and the situation of every soul in it.

This stage of Christ's coming will be a full-scale revelation of His Person in the clouds. He will appear surrounded by those whom He has raised from the dead and the living ones whom He has translated in the Rapture. In this stage every eye shall see Him. It will be a revelation of Christ the Person to the entire human race as He comes to the earth to fight the Battle of Armageddon. This is a final battle between the forces led by the Antichrist and his millions. Jesus Christ shall destroy them with the brightness of His glory. Then He shall return to Jerusalem and there the saints shall crown Him King of Kings and Lord of Lords forever more.

So we have on the one hand the Rapture of the saints, and

on the other, the Revelation of Christ coming back with the saints to rule on the earth. The Rapture is secret. The Revelation of Jesus is public. The Rapture is a moment of time. The Revelation will take place very slowly and universally. In the Rapture, He is coming *for* the saints. In the Revelation, He is coming *with* the saints. In the Rapture, He is coming to catch up the saints out of a wicked world. In the Revelation, He is coming with those saints to rule the world. In the Rapture, He is coming to translate and to resurrect the bodies of the saints of God of all ages. In the Revelation, those same saints are coming with Him to rule with Him forever and ever.

Consider again the significant phrase: "every eye." It means universality of the awesome event; it spells individuality. It is a cosmic and world-shaking event to which none can remain cold nor indifferent. Men of all ages, conditions and countries from Eden's Adam to the last of woman born; souls of all social strata and grades and intellectual capacities; high or low, rich or poor are inescapably and vitally concerned in this stupendous event; for they shall all see Him and see Him immediately. Modern believers see Him through a glass, dimly and representatively, through the study of His words, through the practices of His holy ordinances and through the ministry of God-ordained and Spirit-filled servants. But then "we shall see Him as He is"—face to face. It shall not be a partial view, or a mere passing aspect, like Moses had of God on majestic Sinai, but His full-orbed Person will rest complete on every eyeball. What an irresistible and impressive sight it shall be when He is seen in all His glory! This mortal sphere, this universe has never seen such scenes before.

Far away in the ethereal regions, an uncommon, but faint and undefined brightness begins to appear. But conjecture is sure to give way to certainty—awful, appalling certainty. While they gaze, the appearance which had excited their curiosity rapidly approaches, and still more rapidly brightens. Some may begin to suspect what it may prove, but scarcely any dare to give utterance to their suspicions. Meanwhile the light of the sun begins to fade before a brightness superior to its own. Thousands see their shadows cast in a new direction, and thousands of hitherto careless eyes look up at once to discover the cause. Full clearly they see it, and now new hopes and fears begin to agitate their hearts. The afflicted and long persecuted servants of Christ begin to hope that the predicted, long-expected day of their deliverance is arrived. The wicked, the careless, the unbelieving, begin to fear that the Bible is about to prove no idle tale. And now, fiery shapes, moving like streams of lightning, begin to appear indistinctly amidst the bright dazzling cloud which comes rushing down as on the wings of a whirlwind. At length it reaches its destined place; it pauses—then suddenly unfolding, discloses at once the man Christ Jesus, resplendent in all the glories of the Godhead. Every eye sees him, every heart knows him. Full well do the wretched unprepared inhabitants of the earth now know what to expect; and one universal shriek of anguish and despair rises to heaven, and is echoed back to earth. But louder, far louder than the universal cry, now sounds the last trumpet; and far above all is heard the Omnipotent summoning the dead to arise and come forth from their graves. New terrors await the living. On every side, nay, under their very feet, the earth is in convulsions; graves open, and the dead come forth. Meanwhile, legions of angels are seen descending from pole to pole, gathering together the faithful servants of Christ from the four winds of heaven, and bearing them aloft to meet the Lord in the air, where he causes them to be placed at his own right hand, preparatory to the sentence which is to award them everlasting life.

Such will be the manner of Christ's approach, that every nation and every individual on the globe will see his glory at once; as if two suns should approach our earth at two opposite points, the whole would be irradiated with an ocean of circumambient light, so the Son of Man, with his hosts of mighty angels, in great glory shall come in the clouds of heaven. A trumpet shall sound, and roll its charming notes all round the globe, like deep and jarring thunder; but in it the blessed sound, a still small voice shall cry, and pierce the deep, "Ye dead, arise! my sons, arise! come forth to life eternal."

Then shall the prayer of the militant church, which she had prayed some thousand years, crying, "How long, O Lord, ere thou shalt take the kingdom and possess it forever?" be answered; for lo! he cometh with clouds, with hosts, with millions of saints made perfect, and flaming ministers in his train, to begin the long-predicted reign of righteousness, on earth, and in spirit and in power be present with his spouse a thousand years, and to restore the place of her rest to its ancient splendor and security. Joys unknown before then will roll a tide of bliss over the ravished souls of all his saints all round the globe. At once a shout is heard to rise and float upon the viewless winds, saying, Hallelujah to God in the highest; lo, yonder he comes! it is Jesus himself! I know it is he—the once buffeted God, the formerly slighted Saviour.

Doom of the Beast and the False Prophet

And I saw heaven opened, and behold a white horse; and he that sat upon him was called Faithful and True, and in righteousness he doth judge and make war.

His eyes were as a flame of fire, and on his head were many crowns; and he had a name written, that no man knew, but he himself.

And he was clothed with a vesture dipped in blood: and his name is called the Word of God.

And the armies which were in heaven followed him upon white horses, clothed in fine linen, white and clean.

And out of his mouth goeth a sharp sword, that with it he should smite the nations: and he shall rule them with a rod of iron: and he treadeth the winepress of the fierceness and wrath of Almighty God.

And he hath on his vesture and on his thigh a name written, KING OF KINGS AND LORD OF LORDS.

And I saw an angel standing in the sun; and he cried with a loud voice, saying to all the fowls that fly in the midst of heaven, Come and gather yourselves together unto the supper of the great God;

That ye may eat the flesh of kings, and the flesh of captains, and the flesh of mighty men, and the flesh of horses, and of them that sit on them, and the flesh of all men, both bond and free, both small and great.

And I saw the beast, and the kings of the earth, and their armies, gathered together to make war against him that sat on the horse, and against his army.

And the beast was taken, and with him the false prophet that wrought miracles before him, with which he deceived them that had received the mark of the beast, and them that worshipped his image. These both were cast alive into a lake of fire burning with brimstone (Rev. 19:11-20).

And I saw an angel come down from heaven, having the key to the bottomless pit and a great chain in his hand.

And he laid hold on the dragon, that old serpent, which is the Devil, and Satan, and bound him a thousand years,

And cast him into the bottomless pit, and shut him up and set a seal upon him, that he should deceive the nations no more, till the thousand years should be fulfilled: and after that he must be loosed a little season.

And I saw thrones, and they sat upon them, and judgment was given unto them: and I saw the souls of them that were beheaded for the witness of Jesus, and for the word of God, and which had not worshipped the beast, neither his image, neither had received his mark upon their foreheads, or in their hands; and they lived and reigned with Christ a thousand years.

But the rest of the dead lived not again until the thousand years were finished. This is the first resurrection: ... on such the second death hath no power, but they shall be priests of God and of Christ, and shall reign with him a thousand years (Rev. 20:1-6).

The Judgment of the Nations

When the Son of man shall come in his glory, and all the holy angels with him, then shall he sit upon the throne of his glory:

And before him shall be gathered all nations: and he shall separate them one from another, as a shepherd divideth his sheep from the goats: (St. Matt. 25:31-32).

And these shall go away into everlasting punishment: but the righteous into life eternal (St. Matt. 25:46).

Here we must be very careful not to confuse this judgment with that of the Great White Throne. Here there is no Resurrection; no books are opened; three classes are present—SHEEP, GOATS and Brethren. The time is at the return of Christ (St. Matt. 25:31) and the scene is on the earth (Zech. 14:4). The test in this judgment accorded by the nations to those whom Christ calls "MY BRETHREN." These brethren are the Jewish remnant who will have preached the Gospel of the Kingdom to all nations during the Tribulation.

It is at this crowning triumph and victory of The King of Kings, and Lord of Lords over the beast, Antichrist, captains, kings and nations—the rejectors of the Ominpotent God—that the Jews receive Christ as their One and true Messiah who now begins His Millennial Reign: for the Lord God Omnipotent reigneth!

> Hark! ten thousand harps and voices
>   Sound the praise above;
> Jesus reigns and heaven rejoices,
>   Jesus reigns the God of love;
> See He sits on yonder throne;
>   Jesus rules the world alone.
>
> King of glory, reign forever,
>   Thine an everlasting crown,
> Nothing from Thy love shall sever
>   Those whom Thou hast made Thine own;
> Happy objects of Thy grace,
>   Destined to behold Thy face.
>   Alleluia, Alleluia, Amen.

140

XII

THE KINGDOM OF HOLY MILLENNIUM

The word, millennium, is not recorded in the Bible, but it refers to ideas founded upon it. It denotes a term of a thousand years and in a theological sense the thousand years mentioned in the previous passage in the book of Revelation during which Satan is described as being bound,

> And cast . . . into the bottomless pit, and shut him up, and set a seal upon him, that he should deceive the nations no more, till the thousand years should be fulfilled (Rev. 20:3).

and Christ and saints as reigning triumphant. During this reign of Christ on earth, so long under the tyranny of Satan, and unjust and corrupt rule of man, the world will be under the righteous rule of King of Kings and Lord of Lords Himself. The curse which was pronounced in the Garden of Eden, "cursed be the ground for thy sake," will be removed from the vegetable kingdom. This reign, as already noted, is to last a thousand years, a millennium, "a chilliad." Any thousand years in the calendar of time is a millennium; but because of the apocalyptic peculiarities and preeminence of this particular thousand years, it has been recognized in the canons of the Church as the Millennium. This period of "a thousand years," dates from the overthrow of the Antichrist and his confederates, in the battle of the great day of God Almighty, the casting of him and the False Prophet into the lake of fire, and the binding and locking up of Satan in the Abyss.

In our treatment of the postmillennial theory or Whitby hypothesis, we touched the popular and prevailing modern philosophy that the world is to progress, and is progressing toward a golden age of wisdom, righteousness and peace, when error, vice, wickedness oppression and all antichristianism will be effectually eradicated, and all nations and peoples brought under all-controlling Christianity; that this is to be accomplished by the gradual advancement of science, civilization, reforms, political revolutions, the spread of Christian principles, and the revival of the Churches, and missionary zeal, helped by increased measures of the Spirit of God. Such providential directions of human affairs is the consummation for which all Christians are to look, labor and pray, as the glorious outcome of this world's history. This, men call, Millennium, and about this they dream, sing and preach. That this involves some dim elements of truth, let us admit; but they are so disfigured: there is no beauty that we should desire of them, nothing to be worthy for an article of faith, wholly unknown to the Church in the first thousand years of its existence. In no respectable creed of Christendom is there an entrance and evidence of a manmade Millennium. All the great confessions of Church Fathers, including Reformation giants and theologians are averse to it.

The late Reverend Dr. Reinhold Niebuhr was an eminent and a distinguished American theologian and philosopher of ethics. As architect of a complex philosophy, he combined classical capacities. He rejected utopianism by fallible man and stressed the absurdity and folly of human pretensions; that increase of reason, education, knowledge and technical conquest of nature make for moral progress. It was idolatry, he thought, to suggest that human beings could blueprint and usher in the Kingdom of God on the earth. In the spirit of his Lord and Master, who predicted catastrophe for the end time, theologian Niebuhr had mounting doubts about the inevitability of a millennium through human progress.

And the Lord shall be King over all the earth; in that day shall there be one Lord, and his name one (Zech. 14:9).

142

Thy kingdom come, thy will be done in earth as it is in heaven (St. Matt. 6:10).

And he shall judge among the nations, and shall rebuke many people: and they shall beat their swords into plowshares, and their spears into pruning hooks: nation shall not lift up sword against nation, neither shall they learn war anymore.

The wilderness and the solitary place shall be glad for them: and the desert shall rejoice, and blossom as the rose.

It shall blossom abundantly, and rejoice even with joy and singing: the glory of Lebanon shall be given unto it, the excellency Carmel and Sharon, they shall see the glory of the LORD, and the excellency of our God.

For, behold, I create new heavens and a new earth: and the former shall not be remembered, nor come into mind.

But be ye glad and rejoice forever in that which I create: for behold, I create Jerusalem a rejoicing, and her people a joy.

And I will rejoice in Jerusalem, and joy in my people: and the voice of weeping shall no more be heard in her, nor the voice of crying.

There shall be no more thence an infant of days, nor an old man that hath not filled his days: for the child shall die an hundred years old; but the sinner being an hundred years old shall be accursed.

And they shall build houses, and inhabit them; and they shall plant vineyards, and eat the fruit of them.

They shall not build, and another inhabit; they shall not plant, and another eat: for as the days of a tree are the days of my people. and mine elect shall long enjoy the work of their hands.

They shall not labor in vain, nor bring forth trouble; for they are the seed of the blessed of the LORD, and their offspring with them.

And it shall come to pass, that before they call, I will answer; and while they are yet speaking, I will hear.

The wolf and the lamb shall feed together and the lion shall eat straw like the bullock: and dust shall be the serpent's meat. They shall not hurt nor destroy in all my holy mountain, saith the LORD (Isaiah 2:4, 35:1-2, 65:17-25).

In that day shall there be upon the bells of the horses, HOLINESS UNTO THE LORD; and the pots in the Lord's house shall be like the bowls before the altar.
Yea, every pot in Jerualem and in Judah shall be holiness unto the LORD of hosts: and all they that sacrifice shall come and take of them, and seethe therein: and in that day there shall be no more the Canaanite in the house of the LORD of hosts (Zech. 14:20-21).

The nature and the quality in the animal kingdom shall be changed. All poisonous insects and dangerous beasts shall no longer be a terror.

The wolf also shall dwell with the lamb, and the leopard shall lie down with the kid; and the calf and the young lion and the fatling together; and a little child shall lead them.
And the cow and the bear shall feed; their young ones shall lie down together: and the lion shall eat straw like the ox.
And the sucking child shall play on the hole of the asp, and the weaned child shall put his hand on the cockatrice' den (Isaiah 11:6-8).

War, worrisome and woeful, impossible to reduce to any semblance of logic or morality, will disappear from the face of the earth and the race will be emancipated from its curse, for "he maketh war cease to the end of the earth and he burneth the chariots in fire" (Ps. 46:9). Poverty that patrols and with deep bites stings savagely, breeding ill health and despair, turning ghettos into social sepulchres, will be abolished, sickness and death will be done away with and long life enjoyed by the antediluvian saints will return as in the dawn of creation. The unity of language which was broken at Babel will be restored and the curse and confusion will be forgotten. These thrilling changes which we have been naming, as noted before, operate during Christ's reign on His throne in Jerusalem as the capital of the world with the saints as His assistants. Evil and wrongs are suppressed and righteousness is universally triumphant. The vast cloud of witnesses which no one can number will behold His glory and majesty forever.

> And they sung a new song, saying, Thou art worthy to take the book, and to open the seals thereof: for thou wast slain, and hast redeemed us to God by thy blood out of every kindred, and tongue, and people, and nation;
> And hast made us unto our God kings and priests: and we shall reign on the earth.
> And I beheld, and I heard the voice of many angels round about the throne and the beast and the elders: and the number of them was ten thousand times ten thousand, and thousands of thousands;
> Saying with a loud voice, Worthy is the Lamb that was slain to receive power, and riches, and wisdom, and strength, and honour, and glory, and blessing.
> And every creature which is in heaven, and on the earth, and under the earth, and such as are in the sea, and all that are in them, heard I saying, Blessing, and honour, and glory, and power, be unto him that sitteth upon the throne, and unto the Lamb for ever and ever (Rev. 5:9-13).

Millennium commences—the clouds are dispersed—the heavenly city descends in ineffable splendor—the hosts of contending nations are dispersed—war is heard no more—the world, which for 6,000 years has been stained and darkened with human blood, becomes a scene of peace and prosperity— the feeble government of earthly monarchs is succeeded by the wise and irresistible government of Christ; and the influence of his divine presence spreads abroad throughout all nature, and penetrates unseen into all the dark retreats of misery and crime. A heavenly character refines and elevates the thoughts and actions of mankind; and a frequent communication with heavenly beings affords a perpetual source of wonder and delight. Great objects are daily present to the eyes and to the mind of man, and thus man becomes elevated in thought and

145

lofty in his conceptions, beyond even the records of the earliest ages—and holiness to the Lord, in place of earthly pride, is written upon all the history of each succeeding generation. The history of mankind becomes, for the first time, a part of the history of heaven. And in all this we ourselves may have our part, and in the very highest sphere; whether raised at the First Resurrection, or glorified, while still alive, at the coming of the Lord. In either case, every true believer may have his part in the reign of Christ, and in the glories of the millennial kingdom; not as an inhabitant of the earth, but as a Viceroy of Jesus Christ, ruling over the world, from the golden palaces of the heavenly city.

This will be the time of the complete development of spiritual worship and of Christian civilization in which the shining forth of a more intense and pure light, science, art, industry and commerce will lend their resources to the Christian spirit to enable it to incarnate itself completely in the life of man. Then will be fulfilled the image of the leaven which leaveneth the whole lump. The imperfection of the present universe, which resulted from sin, will be removed; heaven and earth will again appear in pristine beauty and full-orbed glory.

John A. T. Robinson, Bishop of Woolwich, who was referred to previously in this work, has been characterized as a "most lucid and trustworthy theological Virgil," in his "refusal to accept" the infallibility of the Holy Scriptures, the fundamental stress of Christian orthodoxy and eschatology. In his book, *In the End God,* he sums up fancifully:

> The Second Coming has happened in the return of Christ in the Spirit; the Resurrection of the Body has occurred in the putting on of the new man in the Body of Christ; the Millennium has been inaugurated in the reign of Christ in His Church on earth; the Antichrist is a present reality wherever final refusal meets the Christian preaching; the Messianic Banquet is celebrated whenever

the wine is drunk new in the kingdom of God; Satan falls from heaven as each man decides for the Gospel, and in the finished work of Christ the Prince of this world has been judged; the Last Judgment is being wrought out in every moment of choice and decision; Christ is all in all, since all things have been reconciled in Him.

This appears to be mere fancy work—"wood, hay and stubble"—and obscurations of the truth of God. Any theologian who proceeds on such arbitrary and stilted theories and on the assumption and supposition that Christ has already returned in the Person of the Holy Spirit, and then considers this an exhaustive fulfillment of His prediction respecting His future coming in person in a visible form and in the body, is lacking in sound Biblical scholarship and therefore also lacking in credibility. He is monumentally mistaken! Thus his work seems to merit no serious consideration as a "trustworthy" student in depth. Such interpretations, in spite of the glowing descriptions of His return recorded in the Holy Scriltpures, forget that Christ clearly spoke of His eschatological coming; His coming at the end of the ages which is apocalyptically known as His Second Coming. This writer therefore arraigns the above theory as full of Chilliastic error, and as one of those subtle, plausible, but delusive insinuations of the great deceiver, by which God's people are beguiled from the truth to his ruinous lies. The Bible repeatedly speaks of our Lord and Saviour as still in the future;—a great and all comprehensive advent and event long after the outpouring of the Holy Spirit on the day of Pentecost. Apostle Paul, "the most lucid and trustworthy theologian" in all ages of the Church, inerrantly carries the divine dialogue, emphasizing the future appearance of the great God and our Saviour Jesus Christ (Titus 2:13). This is not merely in a manifestation in the Spirit and in the inner life, but a physical, corporal coming, that is, coming in the body. Any other view and explanation such as the one above is a travesty on the plain teachings of the Scriptures. This is not sanctifying the Scriptures, but subverting them.

> To the law and to the testimony: if they speak not according to this word, it is because there is no light in them (Isaiah 8:20).

"He who knows a thing is right," said Pericles in his defense before the Athenian Assembly, "but does not explain it with clearness, is no better than if he had never had a conception of it." No better explanation can be made of the bishop's exuberant fancy and unbridled imagination—a thoroughly untenable hypothesis.

Another eminent ecclesiastic, Bishop Boyd Carpenter, points out: "To an Irenaeus, a Polycarp, a Justin Martyr, a Tertullian, whose eyes were accustomed to the darkness of heathenism, the picture of the world during Christian centuries would have the aspect of a millennium when contrasted with the age of Pagan dominion. But this is only an approximate realization and falls short of the ideal picture. Christendom established and heathenism overthrown would be a millennium in the eyes of Ignatius; but the Church of today looks for a further and higher fulfillment. She can accept the first fruits of God's promises, but she will not mistake them for the harvest; she can rejoice in the Lord's Kingdom, but she looks for the day when the power of evil will be more effectually curbed and the Gospel will have freer course. Then the fulness of Christ's victory will be more clearly seen."

XIII

THE TRIBUNAL OF THE GREAT WHITE THRONE

And I saw a great white throne, and him that sat on it, from whose face the earth and the heaven fled away; and there was found no place for them.

And I saw the dead, small and great, stand before God; and the books were opened: and another book was opened, which is the book of life: and the dead were judged out of those things which were written in the books, according to their works.

And the sea gave up the dead which were in it; and death and hell delivered up the dead which were in them: and they were judged every man according to their works.

And death and hell were cast into the lake of fire. This is the second death.

And whosoever was not found written in the book of life was cast into the lake of fire (Rev. 20:11-15).

Eminent expositors, ancient and modern, consider the opening of this chapter as referring to an early period of the Christian Church, but there are many equally eminent writers who regard the events as occurring in immediate succession to those foreshown at the close of the preceding chapter. The latter is the view of the author.

The events of a thousand years are:

And, when the thousand years are expired, Satan shall be loosed out of his prison,

And he shall go out to deceive the nations which are in the four quarters of the earth (Rev. 20:7-8).

He gathers Gog and Magog together, a formidable array as

the sand of the sea and invades the camp of the saints about the holy and beloved city, the spiritual Jerusalem, in which the most precious of God's people lodged. After a mighty conflict, short and sharp, Satan is defeated, being bound with a great chain, by an angel from heaven, none other than the Lord Jesus Christ Himself, who said: "The Prince of this world is judged." The Devil, the arch-ringleader in that fearful triumvirate, the Dragon, the wild Beast and the False Prophet—the ecclesiastical minister of Antichrist—is sentenced and sent to ultimate confinement and punishment in the lake of fire. Thus we perceive three distinct personalities; the Devil, the Antichrist and the False Prophet, and these three are one, one vital essence, one economy and one administration. The Dragon sets up as the Anti-God, the ten-horned Beast is the Antichrist, and the two-horned Beast proceeding from and operating in the interest of both is the Anti-Holy Ghost. And these three together are Hell's Trinity in Unity.

> And the devil that deceived them was cast into the lake of fire and brimstone, where the beast and the false prophet are, and shall be tormented day and night forever and ever (Rev. 20:10).

Well may we exclaim in looking ahead to these solemn scenes:

> O the depths of the riches both of the wisdom and knowledge of God! how unsearchable are his judgments, and his ways past finding out! (Romans 11:33).

Satan and all the enemies with whom the Christian Church in all ages was in conflict, have been overthrown and utterly destroyed, and very properly will be called to an account in the Judgment of the Great White Throne which will determine every man's everlasting state.

I charge thee therefore before God, and the Lord Jesus

Christ, who shall judge the quick and the dead at his appearing and his kingdom: (II Tim. 4:1).

It requires no Napoleonic imagination to understand that this will be a great day when all shall appear before the judgment seat of Christ. It was this doctrine "of righteousness and judgment to come," proclaimed in the splendor of the Roman court by Paul the prisoner, the greatest religious genius of all time, that made Felix, the distinguished procurator of Emperor Claudius in Palestine tremble. It was with this cogent reasoning, in sublime strains, grace and majesty that Paul, in defense of his life and experience in the service of his crucified and risen Saviour, confounded the court and orator Tertullus, his accuser.

The solemn scene of Judgment is before the formidable tribunal at the Great White Throne—the throne of glory. There is no name, no figure, no shape, but only an awful, mysterious and composed presence, which can be nothing less than the One, unnamable, indescribable, eternal Godhead. The prophet Isaiah also had an awful and exciting vision of this throne of glory—the glory of Christ too dazzling for mortal vision, that terrified him with judgment in prostration, self-abnegation and conviction before the Holy God. "Woe is me! for I am undone."

In the year that king Uzziah died I saw also the Lord sitting upon a throne, high and lifted up, and his train filled the temple,

Above it stood the seraphims: each one had six wings; with twain he covered his face, and with twain he covered his feet, and with twain he did fly.

And one cried unto another, and said, Holy, holy, holy, is the Lord of hosts: the whole earth is full of his glory.

And the posts of the door moved at the voice of him that cried, and the house was filled with smoke.

Then said I, Woe is me! for I am undone; because I am a man of unclean lips, and I dwell in the midst of a people of unclean lips: for mine eyes have seen the King, the Lord of hosts (Isaiah 6:1-5).

This great white throne, "high and lifted up," not only is above other thrones as it transcends them, but over other thrones as it rules and commands them. The appearance of the judge in his judicial supremacy and dignity is the Lord Jesus Christ Himself, who then puts on such awful holiness and indescribable majesty and terror that the earth and the heaven flee from His face and there is no place found for them. The Lord Jesus Christ is indeed the Judge, to whom all judgment is committed; but He does it under and in the presence of the enthroned Godhead of the Father, the Son, and the Holy Ghost. The throne had the appearance of a reddish crystalline brilliancy like pure flames, attractive even in its awfulness. Here then is nothing but the naked presence of almightiness, so dreadful that the very earth and heaven seem to flee into nothingness before it. The earth and heaven do not literally fly away and disappear. This is simply the intensification of the description of the awfulness and majesty of the occupant upon the throne signifying that almightiness by which all the creations and changes in the universe are effected, and who here assumes his eternal power to dispose of his enemies forever and inaugurates the renewal and "re-genesis" of his Creation. The classes and persons to be judged, the dead, small and great; that is, young and old, high or low, rich and poor; none are so great and powerful as to bribe the judge or avoid the jurisdiction of this Supreme Court. The order of events begins with the resurrection of the impenitent and unrepentant and unsaved dead. The resurrection of the saved occurred at the Parousia or the Rapture, when Christ came for His saints. Of them it is written: "Blessed and holy is he that hath part in the first resurrection" (Rev. 20:6). "But the rest of the dead lived not again until the thousand years were finished" (Rev. 20:5). Now they emerge from their graves, both small and great, and they stand before Christ the

Judge. "For the Father judgeth no man, but hath committed all judgment unto the Son" (John 5:22).

The rule of judgment is conducted by the open books—the book of God's omniscience, who is greater than man's consciences and knows all things, for there is a book of remembrance with him both for good and evil; and the book of sinner's conscience, which though formerly secret will now be opened. This means that heaven keeps record of all human deeds, thoughts, feelings and acts. Myriads of men have lived and died of whom the world knows nothing; but the lives they lived, the deeds they wrought, the thoughts and tempers they indulged, still stand written where the memory of them cannot perish. Not a human being has ever breathed earth's atmosphere whose career is not traced at full length in the book's eternity. The eminent preacher Dr. Joseph Fort Newton, whose fascinating biography, *River of Years,* has received wide attention and reading, in a unique discourse said: "Everybody should write their own biography." Though few will measure up to this standard in the life that now is, whoever we might be, our biography is written in heaven. An unerring hand has recorded every item, with every secret thing, good or bad, there described in bold letters, by its true name, and set down to individual account, to be brought forth for final settlement, if not entirely blotted out through the blood of Christ before this life of ours is ended. And if no other books are to be thought of, the book of your own conscience, and the book of God's remembrance, will then and there attest one's every misdeed and ill-dessert. Think, ye that fear not God and make nothing of trampling His laws, how your case will stand when those books are opened!

While these pages were receiving their final touches, United Press International of Hartford, Connecticut, recalled a Dark Day on its 191st anniversary that frightened New England. Though the unforgettable day—May 19, 1780, dawned clear and warm, by noon the atmospheric heavens were shrouded in pitch-blackness. For fourteen frightening hours many New

Englanders thought Judgment Day had arrived.

Worried residents carried torches in the streets. Candles could be seen inside homes. Schoolmasters dismissed classes. Merchants closed shops. Churches opened their doors.

At the state capital in Hartford where legislators seldom have been shaken since, there was a fearless cry in the House of Representatives. "Mr. Speaker," said a member from Stamford, Colonel Abraham Davenport, "this well may be the Day of Judgment which the world awaits. With all reverence, I would say, 'Let God do His work, we'll do ours!' " A Boston minister, the Reverend Mather Byles, was asked by a parishioner what could cause such a phenomenon. The minister replied that he was "as much in the dark" as everybody else. At Bath, Maine, a ship's carpenter fell overboard due to the darkness. He was rescued. In Vermont, written accounts indicate "the birds, having sung their evening songs, disappeared and were silent; roosters crowed as at daybreak."

Referring to the "dark day" many years later, poet John Greenleaf Whittier wrote that "men prayed and women wept, all ears sharp to hear the doom-blast of the trumpet shatter the sky."

But no horn of Gabriel blew. A full moon was due to rise at nine o'clock that evening, and relief etched the faces of the worried when at 1 A.M. the moon peeped through the blackness, high and red as blood. The sun rose reassuringly next morning, and for New England it was business as usual.

But one of these days, it will not be business as usual for New England, for America and for the vengeful and apostate world.

> And all the host of heaven shall be dissolved, and the heavens shall be rolled together as a scroll: and all their host shall fall down, as the leaf falleth off from the vine, and as a falling fig from the fig tree.
> For my sword shall be bathed in heaven: (Isaiah 34:4-5).

Of the justice and grace of God we are made aware when

the angel, swift minister of judgment, spreads his wings over the world. In the darkened sky there is a crash as if the vast canopy of the firmament were torn asunder. And now a keen flash lights the gloom for a moment; anon it is swallowed up, as if the inverted sea poured in cataracts upon the flame extinguishing it. Man recognizes the divine indignation and even the beasts of the field seem to be aware. The sound comes as it were out of the mouth of God, reverberating from sky to earth and from earth to sky and rolling away under the whole heaven.

> Can any understand the spreading of the cloud,
> The crashing of His pavilion?
> Behold He spreadeth His light about Him;
> And covereth it with the depths of the sea,
> For by these judgeth He the people.

God will create new heavens and a new earth.

> For, behold, I create new heavens and a new earth: for the former shall not be remembered, nor come into mind (Isaiah 65:17).

This new home, saith the Lord of the redeemed, "not made with hands, in the heavens," will be untarnished by sin and will be a place worthy of the Bride of Christ. Happy and blessed are those who have ordered their lives according to God's ways and Word. They shall be justified in the great day of the Lord!

After the final judgment when "The Kingdoms of this world are become the Kingdom of our Lord and His Christ, He shall have delivered up the Kingdom to God, even the Father" (I Cor. 15:24). Henceforth, God shall be all in all; preparing the saints for the final and eternal state of the redeemed in heaven. Hallelujah!

The apocalyptic text above reminds us that there is

"another book, which is that of the book of life"—the register of the washed and sanctified through faith in the redeeming blood of Jesus Christ. This book too must be opened and its testimony brought into the decision: for many there be whose lives are fair and honest, conscientious and morally irreproachable, who have fulfilled all the requirements of law and virtue, like the rich young ruler of Biblical fame, but like him have never experienced the regenerating power of the new creation by a personal surrender to Jesus Christ as Lord and Saviour. Exemplary as they may have been in their own goodness and morality, "All these things have I kept from my youth up": they have not believed on the only begotten Son of God, and therefore have not life, and so are not written in the book of life. He alone hath earned the right to an evelasting life who hath believed "on the Son" (St. John 3:36).

> And I saw the dead, small and great, stand before God; and the books were opened: and another book was opened, which is the book of life: and the dead were judged out of those things which were written in the books, according to their works (Rev. 20:12).
> And whosoever was not found written in the book of life was cast into the lake of fire (Rev. 20:15).
> Then shall he say also unto them on the left hand, Depart from me, ye cursed, into everlasting fire, prepared for the devil and his angels (St. Matt. 25:41).

And another book shall be opened—the book of the Holy Scriptures, the statute-book of heaven, the rule of life. "Forever, O LORD, thy word is settled in heaven" (Ps. 119:89). This book is opened as containing the law, the touchstone by which the hearts and lives of men are to be tried. This book determines the matter of right; the other books give evidence of matters of faith.

The cause to be tried is the works of man, what they have done and whether it be good or evil. By their works men shall be justified or condemned before a righteous God. The issue of the trial and judgment will be according to the evidence of fact and rule of judgment. All those who have made a covenant with death and an agreement with hell shall then be condemned with their infernal confederates; cast with them into a lake of fire. "This shall be the portion of their cup." According to the rules and verdict of the infallible Scriptures, Christ shall judge the secrets of all men according to the Gospel. Sin is alienation from God; hell is the realization of that alienation. The punishment of the alienated sinners on the unimpeachable authority of God's Word is everlasting. For if anyone be not found written in the Book of Life, he is destined to be swallowed up by the Lake of Fire. And He, who understands it best calls it "a lake of fire and brimstone." The rapid consummation of history and of the physical universe follows the judgment (Rev. 21:1). Throughout the long history of the human race, the earth and the world have been the scene and seat of "the lust of the flesh, the lust of the eyes, and the pride of life"—SIN. "This world which was not of the Father is destined for utter destruction" (II Peter 3:10).

In the conduct of Divine Providence towards the Church in the world, and according to the perfection, pattern and sanctity of the Holy Scriptures as a revelation from God, the most sublime philosophy of any in profane history, we have considered the Doctrine of His promise, "I will come again" as the Second Coming of the Lord Jesus Christ; the promised Messiah of the Old Testament, the offspring of David, the life and light of the world. We have defined what Christ's Coming is; this was followed with the citation of the prophetic witnesses of His Second Coming; in the next step we considered the time of His Coming; the fourth embraced the seven intensifying signs of His Coming. To the questions, why the Lord delayeth His Coming and why will He come, we have presented cogent and convincing Scriptural reasons. The seventh step reads: when the Lord cometh—what? Theologically speaking, chapters eight through twelve: Rapture, the Great Tribulation, the Millennium, the Day of Divine

Judgment and finally Heaven; these particularly, fall within the orbit of eschatology—the doctrine of final events immediately preceding Christ's return from heaven.

XIV

A NEW HEAVEN

And I saw a new heaven and a new earth: for the first heaven and the first earth were passed away; and there was no more sea.

And I John saw the holy city, new Jerusalem, coming down from God out of heaven, prepared as a bride adorned for her husband.

And I heard a great voice out of the heaven saying, Behold, the tabernacle of God is with men, and he will dwell with them, and they shall be his people, and God himself shall be with them, and be their God.

And God shall wipe away all tears from their eyes; and there shall be no more death, neither sorrow, nor crying, neither shall there be any more pain: for the former things are passed away.

And he that sat upon the throne said, Behold, I make all things new. And he said unto me, Write: for these words are true and faithful.

And he said unto me, It is done. I am Alpha and Omega, the beginning and the end. I will give unto him that is athirst of the fountain of the water of life freely.

He that overcometh shall inherit all things; and I will be his God, and he shall be my son.

But the fearful, and unbelieving, and the abominable, and murderers, and whoremongers, and sorcerers, and idolators, and all liars, shall have their part in the lake which burneth with fire and brimstone: which is the second death (Rev. 21:1-8).

In the final two chapters of the apocalypse—the book of Revelation, there are two monosyllables that remarkably describe future and heaven. They are "no" and "new." Most significantly, each is mentioned seven times, the symbol of moral perfection and protection. "No death, no earthly temple, no sun, no defilement, no curse, no night, no candle." Behold, I make all things new. New heaven, new earth, new Jerusalem, new people, new things, new Temple, new light.

A new Heaven. "A new Heaven" does not mean that the old heaven such as we had known is swept out of existence, but it is retouched and renovated, cleansed and brightened up from its old disorders and imperfections. The heaven over us now, in its present operation is indeed most beneficent and inspiring. How beautiful and blessed the never ceasing procession of the majestic sun, "which is as a bridegroom coming out of his chamber, whose going forth is from the end of the heaven . . . and there is nothing hid from the heat thereof." In the moon and stars and clouds and ritual of seasons, days and nights and showers too, "the heavens declare the glory of God: . . . There is no speech nor language, where their voice is not heard." What will that new investment be to which the present creation is to give place! "We cannot describe the meteorology of that new heaven," says Dr. Seiss, the eminent apocalyptist, "but it will be a heaven which no more robes itself in angry tempests and menacing blackness, . . . nor gives working place to the Devil and his angels. We often look at the blue sky that watches over us, at the rosy morning's welcome to the king of day; . . . at the mellow glories of the setting sun; at the solemn midnight lit all over with its twinkling star gems, and we are thrilled with Jehovah's works. What, then, shall it be when the Great Architect, set to do honor to the love and faithfulness of His only begotten Son, shall put forth His hand upon it the second time, to renew it in a fresh and eternal splendor." These are the abiding characteristics of heaven, great in their signification; but the greatest of them is that there shall be no more death, no more diseased bodies, wracked with pain; for our resurrection-bodies will be like our Lord's resurrection-body. We are new people: "Beloved, now are the sons of God," the citizens of New Jerusalem. There will be no temples nor ornate cathedrals made by mortal hands, for the Lord God Almighty and the Lamb are the temple of it (Rev. 21:22). Every exercise and act of service of the redeemed will be holiness unto the Lord. The proud Lucifer, son of the morning, who boasted, "I will exalt my throne above the stars of God: I will ascend above the heights of the clouds; I will be like the most High"; the prince of this world which weakened the nations, made the earth to tremble and shook the kingdoms and turned the world into a wilderness; all of his pomp and pageantry is finally brought down to the grave. The archenemy of God and man with his inventive genius of curse, sin and hell is now forever cast out and brought down to hell.

And a New Earth. The old earth is now in deep captivity to corruption, and homestead of the human race, where the miseries of a deep, dark and universal apostasy from God holds sway. Imagine, then what its regeneration must bring: an earth which no longer smarts and smokes under the curse of sin—an earth where thorns and thistles do not infest the ground, nor reptiles hiss among the flowers of Eden, nor savage beasts lie in ambush to devour—an earth whose sod is never marred with graves, whose soil is never bedewed with tears nor profaned with warriors' blood, whose fields and productive acres are never blasted with hurricanes and unpropitious seasons and droughts, whose atmosphere never gives wings to the seeds of plagues and death, whose ways are never lined with funeral processions—an earth whose hills ever flow with salvation, and whose valleys know only the benignity of the Creator's smiles—an earth from end to end, and from center to utmost verge, clothed with the eternal beauty and blessedness of Paradise Restored!—an earth restored to the creation's first day: "and God saw that it was good," sublimely good.

The New Jerusalem. The Holy City, the House of God fresh from heaven, will be the universal capital of the new earth in surpassing splendor, glory and infinite Majesty; a creation of

God's unbounded wisdom, power and love; never before conceived by the mind of mortal men. How incomparably excellent is the glory of heaven where no change shall be; advancement without injustice; abundance of glory, but without envy; infinite wealth, but without woe; admirable beauty and felicity, but without vanity and infirmity. The hymns, songs and anthems which give limitless room to the understanding, and swell the oratorio with ever increasing hallelujahs and praise are ever new. Here, we live, move and have our being, forever viewing bliss so great, the glory of the crowned and enthroned Lamb with the effulgence of the Godhead so ineffable; it is at once a sinless splendor! Here we are partakers of eternal consolations, bathed in the radiant smiles of our Redeemer King with never-fading "palms of victory" in our hands and ever-shining robes with ever-thrilling songs and ever-flowing hallelujahs on our tongues. Here we are with joy-speaking eyes which never weep, lips which never thirst and uplifted hands, like the High Priest pontificating at the Altar in the Holy of Holiest, who never tires. Here sorrow and sighing shall flee away!

"It doth not yet appear what we shall be"; but as golden crowns exceed palm branches, and kings are above servants, and the possession of a throne is more than to stand before one, even by so much is the heavenly estate held out to us the children of God.

> I know not, O I know not
> What royal joys are there!
> What radiancy of glory
> What life beyond compare!

The eternal blessedness of the City of God and Kingdom of Christ in heaven, will not consist merely in the absence of "No's" of earthly woes, and presence of "New's." The glory of heaven is comprehended in this, that the redeemed saints "shall see His face, and tell the story saved by Grace!" while

His name adorns their foreheads. Our eternity will be spent in His presence and company and we shall reign forever and ever while serving Him. It has been said that, "Queen Elizabeth reigns, but does not rule." The King of Kings, and Lord of Lords *reigns and rules,* and we shall rule with Him. "Do ye not know," reminds the holy apostle, "that the saints shall judge the world?" (I Cor. 6:12). Some high ecclesiastical leaders here on earth have been called "Princes of the Church." We are all princes, priests and kings unto God and unto Him Who loved us and washed us from our sins in His own blood;—to Him be glory and dominion forever and ever throughout all Eternity. Amen.

The high priestly prayer which the Lord Jesus Christ offered in the seventeenth chapter of the Gospel according to Saint John is ultimately and eternally answered: "The glory which thou gavest me, I have given them." Forever and ever the saints shall be heirs of God and joint heirs with Jesus Christ in Heaven.

> Her streets with burnished gold are paved round;
> Stars lie like pebbles scattered on the ground;
> Pearls mixed with Onyx and jasper stone,
> Made gravelled causeway to be trampled on,
> There shines no sun by day, no moon by night,
> The Palace glory is the Palace light;
> There is no time to measure be —
> There time is swallowed in eternity;
> And lumpish sorrow, and degen'rous care,
> Are banished thence, and death's stranger there;
> But simple love and semiternal joys,
> Whose sweetness never gluts, nor fulness cloys:
> Where face to face, our ravished eye shall see,
> Great God, that glorious One in Three.

Another subject, presenting itself to our notice as being part of our heavenly inheritance, is the renewing of the ties of nature and social intercourse. A longing desire to meet again seems to proceed from a source which is part of our nature. But in many instances a doubt hangs over the subject, rendering the hope uncertain, and the parting more painful. Besides, the question, if we do meet again, shall we know each other?, is asked very frequently. This uncertainty does not proceed from want of evidence, but from want of reflection. If there is to be such an identity between the mortal and the glorified body as we are led to expect from Scripture inference, we may venture to believe that the glorified saints will recognize one another, not only through the new and higher powers of the mind, but also by the features of the former mortal body, still traceable in the new and glorified state. This, to judge by our present perception, is indispensable for that enjoyment which is anticipated from meeting and recognizing one another; at least, a very considerable part of the expected joy would be found wanting if dear friends and relatives should meet with features unknown to them.

But that there will be a meeting of friends and relatives, such as will render their joy perfect, may be proved from Scripture. The apostle (I Thess. 4:13, 14), says, "I would not have you ignorant, brethren, concerning them that are asleep, that ye sorrow not, even as others which have no hope. For if we believe that Jesus died and rose again, even so them also which sleep in Jesus will God bring with him." This passage does not refer, in the first place, to the resurrection of the saints, and their coming with Christ, so much as it does to the meeting together and recognizing of friends: for the obvious object of the apostle is to comfort bereaved Christians with the hope that they shall see one another again in the world to come. This seeing each other naturally comprises both meeting and recognition. That of Christ, by his friends after his resurrection, is a proof that no change of features had taken place. We may therefore infer also, from this circumstance, that the features of the mortal body will be distinctly traceable in the glorified body. It is true, and certainly very striking, that at the temporal transfiguration of our Lord upon the

164

Holy mount, the fashion of his countenance was altered, and his raiment became white and glistening; but still this is no proof that the features of his countenance were changed. His face did shine as the sun, assuming that glory in which he appears now, and in which we shall see him at his coming. But it is more than probable that the alteration of his countenance refers only to the glory which beamed from it, even as a splendid dress often beautifies and alters, in some measure, the countenance without changing its features. Moreover, there is no reasonable ground for assuming that the original features of Christ's human countenance, and those of the saints, shall undergo a change.

The Lord Jesus Christ is coming back again! He is the prophet and pledge of His Second Coming; angels are witnesses of His Coming; the believers of all ages beginning from the apostles down to our day preached and proclaimed His glorious return. Are we ready to greet Him, to meet Him, to welcome Him? We are in the midst of mighty and ever-present and ever-intensifying signs of the times, which are John the Baptist and forerunners of His Second Coming. The increase of knowledge, the rapid growth of apostasy, worldwide Evangelism, the rich man, Israel—God's sun dial—Gentile government, Jerusalem, the material earth; these and other cloud of signs are thundering in our anxious ears with no uncertain sounds that our Lord is soon coming. "Blessed are those servants whom the Lord when he cometh shall find watching: Verily I say unto you, that he shall gird himself, and make them to sit down to meat, and will come forth and serve them" (St. Luke 12:37).

Esteemed reader, so that we, "as gods knowing good and evil" may reach our true and glorious destiny in heaven, described above; we must by faith take hold of the coming Christ whose First Coming was to seek and to save that which was least, last and lost. Believe; because you were created to believe. The laws of your mind and heart are the laws of FAITH—man's bridge to Eternity. You cannot deny and remain a moral being sealed with the image and likeness of God. The presence or absence of faith rules the whole destiny of man. Have faith in the Lord your God, the supreme lover of your soul. The soul separated from God is a dying soul, unless some link of love is forged. Christ is that link. Believe on the Lord Jesus Christ, God's answer to the dying soul in a dying world, and thou shalt be saved. So shall you be established— so shall you prosper, even as your soul prospereth for time and Eternity in Heaven.

> In that bright City you would dwell,
> With that blest Church the Saviour praise;
> And safe redeemed from death and hell,
> Sit at His feet through endless days.
> So shall you Eternity thus gain,
> Without these all else is vain.

Tradition has preserved for us an historical legend which describes a maiden whose lover left her for a voyage to the Holy Land, promising upon his return to make her his bride. There were many who told her that she would never see him again. But she believed his word, and so she went down to the lonely shore, and evening after evening kindled there a beacon-light in sight of the roaring waves, to hail and welcome the returning ship which was to bring again her betrothed. And by that watchfire she took her stand every night, praying to the winds to hasten on the sluggish sails, that he who was everything to her might come. Even so our blessed Lord who loved us unto death, has gone away to the heavenly Holy Land, promising upon His return to make us His happy Bride. There be those, who say that He has gone forever, and that we shall never see Him anymore. But His last word was, "I come quickly." And on the dark and misty beach sloping out into the eternal sea, each true believer stands by the love-lit fire, watching and waiting, and praying and hoping for the full-orbed fulfillment of His word, in nothing happier than His pledge and promise, and longing ever from the soul of sacred love, "Even so, come, Lord Jesus." And one of these days, while the world is busy with its gay frivolities and giant problems mocking at the maiden on the shore, a form shall appear over the surging waves as that on Galilee on the first Easter morning, to vindicate forever all this watching and devotion, and bring to the faithful and constant heart a joy—"It is the Lord!"—and glory and triumph which never more shall end.

To alert the indifferent, to awaken the sleeper and unconcerned souls and believingly and intelligently lead to the enviable position and admirable attitude of that memorable maiden, is the intent of this interpretation. And if this survey of the Apocalypse of Jesus Christ has brought my esteemed readers to such love-waiting and watching in these strange and stern days and dark shores of time, all praise be unto Him. All praise be unto Him, from whom has come the grace to set the soul in confident expectation of the speedy fulfillment of the cosmic wonders we have been contemplating—then, I am humbly content to take my leave of this labor.

Friends of God, armed with His arms, watch and endure by an unshakable faith in God. Act with God and act for God! Put away the crepe! Belay those funeral dirges! This may be the time for palm branches and hallelujahs.

To the cheering message of Christ and of His nearing Epiphany, "Surely I come quickly," how exciting it is that Saint John, the rapt apocalyptic seer, the only surviving apostle living upon the earth, in his Patmos Prayer, the last and loftiest of the Holy Bible, in the sublimity of his hope, prays: "Even so, come, Lord Jesus." In today's thundering era of appalling cosmic crisis, with the solemn judgment and sublime sense of the future of our inborn eternity in our thought, may Divine Grace enable us to make this, the most comprehensive and world embracing prayer by the venerable Servant of God, that involves the soul of us all; "EVEN SO, COME, LORD JESUS," our own. This doctrine of the future, my esteemed reader, of sheer necessity, is that each of us must seek his own apocalypse in a vision of life in the union of his spirit with Jesus Christ, the ultimate answer to the questionings and questings of every pure seeker. Jesus came! Jesus died! Jesus rose again! Jesus is coming again! And in Him God has appointed a Day in which He will judge the world in transcendent righteousness which is forever one with Love.

> See the judge our nature wearing,
> Clothed in majesty divine;
> You will long for His appearing
> Then shall say, This God is mine!
> Gracious Saviour,
> Own us in that day as Thine.
> AMEN and AMEN.

THE TWENTY-FOUR ELDERS AND
FOUR CHERUBIM ROUND THE SECOND ADVENT THRONE

(Courtesy of 40 Future Wonders of Descriptive Prophecy)

15 And the seventh angel sounded; and there were great voices in heaven, saying, The kingdoms of this world are become *the kingdoms* of our Lord, and of his Christ; and he shall reign for ever and ever.

16 And the four and twenty elders, which sat before God on their seats, fell upon their faces, and worshipped God.

17 Saying, We give thee thanks, O Lord God Almighty, which art, and wast, and art to come; because thou hast taken to thee thy great power, and hast reigned.

Alleluia: for the Lord God omnipotent reigneth.

A POETICAL DEFINITION
OF
THE LORD JESUS CHRIST'S COMING AGAIN

The Lord Jesus Christ is Coming again
His pledge, His promise, performance fulfill;
This Doctrine was the Hope since time began,
Of Saints for whom He cometh, He will.

Christ's Coming back doth not occur in death,
For Saints and Sinners alike die day by day;
Bodily, in person, "I will come," He saith,
Gird up your loins, be ready, "watch and pray."

'Tis not our going to Him, He comes for us,
'Tis not the Holy Spirit, another is He;
'Tis not Spiritual coming to armor Church thus,
He visibly comes for all eyes to see.

Prophets are witnesses of Christ's return
"This same Jesus shall come," Angels too testified;
Apostles of the Lord wrote each in their turn,
As they saw Him ascend "to God" whom on earth
    He glorified.

Time of Christ's Coming, no mortal doth know,
Only His Heavenly Father, our God alone:
Imminent, at any hour, conqueror every foe,
When God and man shall speak as one.

Signs of Christ's Coming are alive abroad,
Natural, Political, Moral, Commercial too;
Signs and cosmic wonders of Creation's God,
Spiritual, Ecclesiastical, lo, the sign of the Jew!

170

Why the Lord will come again dissenters may ask,
To receive His own to mansions above;
This earthly vow, His heavenlier task
Mingles with God in holiest love.

PAROUSIA—the upward call of Christ in God,
The Church's rapture from earth to heaven;
The Holy path Himself hath trod,
Sublime enjoyment of the forgiven.

REVELATION—Christ shall come in full-orbed glory,
To enthrone His Kingdom on mortal sphere;
This cosmic event crowns Salvation's story,
Salvation with those we hold so dear!

MILLENNIUM—a thousand years of peace,
When sorrow and sighing shall flee away;
The blast of wars shall hush, and parleys cease,
Blind see, deaf hear, dumb shall sing that day.

Oh, on that day, life's reckoning hour,
When man to judgment wakes from clay,
Standeth Son of God ever, our soul's desire,
Though heaven and earth shall pass away.

Make thy choice, esteemed reader, destined as you are
To share the Coming Christ's blessing at your spirit's goal;
"Offspring of David, the bright morning star,"
Receiving the end of your faith, salvation of your soul.